D1588726

ESSENTIAL PSYCHOLOGY

**General Editor
Peter Herriot**

E2

SELECTION AND ASSESSMENT AT WORK

ESSENTIAL

PSYCHOLOGY

SELECTION AND ASSESSMENT AT WORK

Gilbert and Helen Jessup

Methuen

First published 1975 by Methuen & Co Ltd
11 New Fetter Lane, London EC4P 4EE
© 1975 Gilbert Jessup
Printed in Great Britain by
Richard Clay (The Chaucer Press), Ltd
Bungay, Suffolk
ISBN (hardback) 0 416 82260 6
ISBN (paperback) 0 416 82270 3

We are grateful to Grant McIntyre of
Open Books Publishing Ltd for assistance
in the preparation of this series

Contents

Editor's Introduction

Gilbert and Helen Jessup review the vast range of individual differences, both intellectual and personal, which characterize those who work. They evaluate the tools which are used to assess these differences, and show how an awareness of their findings can help a person find a job to which he is suited. Jobs and the organizations which are their context have to be taken into account, and the Jessups conclude by highlighting the rapid changes which will occur in the nature of work, and the consequent adaptability required of the worker.

Unit E of *Essential Psychology* deals with a particular area of applied psychology: psychology and work. This is an ideal topic to demonstrate the ways in which the different psychological models of man and their associated findings can be utilized. The human being as processor of information copes with varied inputs in his job and has to adjust his behaviour accordingly. As a social being, he is much affected by the groups of people with whom he works and the organization within which he operates. As a developing person, his changing view of himself will partly consist of his view of himself at work. As an in-

7

dividual, he brings differing skills and motives to his work. Above all, as a human being, he possesses the capacity to change his work situation to suit his own abilities and objectives.

Essential Psychology as a whole is designed to reflect this changing structure and function of psychology. The authors are both academics and professionals, and their aim has been to introduce the most important concepts in their areas to beginning students. They have tried to do so clearly, but have not attempted to conceal the fact that concepts that now appear central to their work may soon be peripheral. In other words, they have presented psychology as a developing set of views of man, not as a body of received truth. Readers are not intended to study the whole series in order to 'master the basics'. Rather, since different people may wish to use different theoretical frameworks for their own purposes, the series has been designed so that each title stands on its own. But it is possible that if the reader has read no psychology before, he will enjoy individual books more if he has read the introduction (A1, B1 etc.) to the units to which they belong. Readers of the units concerned with applications of psychology (E, F) may benefit from reading all the introductions.

A word about references in the text to the work of other writers – e.g. 'Smith (1974)'. These occur where the author feels he must acknowledge an important concept or some crucial evidence by name. The book or article referred to will be listed in the References (which double as Name Index) at the back of the book. The reader is invited to consult these sources if he wishes to explore topics further.

We hope you enjoy psychology.

Peter Herriot

1
General issues in psychological measurement

Introduction

Quantification or measurement is fundamental to science. Quantification is also essential to rational decision-making in the real world. Our understanding of human behaviour has developed slowly and it is only in recent years that we have begun to get to grips with the problems of motivation, learning, personality and so on. Yet it is only by understanding these phenomena that we can hope to make a reasonable assessment about how people are going to react to different situations. This understanding is required by anyone who is to manage, lead, or otherwise influence other people whether in small work groups, large industrial organizations, in trade unions or in the wider community by social planners and government.

This book is about the measurement of human characteristics and how such measures can be used to make predictions about future behaviour. The practical applications are concerned mainly with people's life at work or in preparation for work. For example, a knowledge of one's own abilities, personality and motivation is invaluable in making decisions about the choice of careers. Far too many people drift into jobs for which they are not suited. Often this is not fully realized until considerable time and effort has been invested in training and gaining experience to perform the job. It is difficult to go back and start again. Psychological tests can provide valuable information to individuals on the types of jobs in which they are likely to succeed and obtain satisfaction. From the employer's point of view psychological assessment can also be most useful in making decisions about who to select for particular jobs. The use of psychological measures in personnel selection has become well accepted practice in most large organizations.

The importance of assessment does not stop at the point of entry to employment but continues throughout working life. Managers require measures of the performance of individuals to monitor their operation and to re-allocate, promote and generally develop the careers of their staff. Managers are also becoming increasingly aware that they need information on the attitudes of their staff in order to manage effectively.

Some of the more progressive organizations are beginning to think of their personnel as an asset in some ways comparable to their capital assets. (One often hears managers say 'our employees are our most valuable asset'.) This is leading to the idea of 'human asset accounting', that is, measuring how much members of staff are worth to the organization. The experienced and more highly trained are in general of greater value. If it is possible to place a value on people's skills it will provide a rational basis upon which to organize recruitment, training and development programmes. We are only beginning to grapple with these problems.

Measuring instruments

There are certain essential properties of good measuring instruments whether they be rulers, weighing machines or tests of intelligence. We take these characteristics so much for granted in the case of rulers, weighing machines and other physical measuring instruments that we seldom bother to consider them. There are also important ways in which measuring instruments differ (see A8).

In the case of rulers and weighing machines we have units of measurement such as centimetres and kilogrammes. What is the unit of intelligence? It is meaningful to say that a man who weighs 100 kilogrammes weighs twice as much as a man of 50 kilogrammes. What does twice as intelligent mean?

The difference between these types of measures are that length, weight and most physical measures have 'absolute' scales of measurement, while intelligence and most psychological characteristics can at best be assessed on a 'normative' scale. That is to say it is only possible to express a person's intelligence as being higher than or lower than another person's intelligence. The scores obtained are only relative and usually expressed in relation to the norm of the general population or some specified sub-population. IQ scores are of this nature and should be interpreted in relation to an average IQ in the general population of 100 and a standard deviation of 15 (see Appendix A to this book and also A8 for fuller explanation.)

Reliability

Another major problem found with psychological measures is that of their 'reliability'. For a test to be reliable in this technical sense, it should measure accurately whatever it is in fact measuring. One way of checking this would be to give a test to the same group of people on two separate occasions. If we ignore the possible effects of practice (i.e.

prior experience of doing the test the first time) on performance on the second occasion we would hope that individuals would get the same score on both occasions. In fact they don't, but with the better tests their second score is of the same order as the first. Thus if a man scores 70 per cent on the first occasion we might expect him to score between, say, 65–75 per cent on the second occasion. If a man took the same intelligence test repeatedly and scored 70, 65, 68 and 74 one could say with some degree of confidence that his 'true' score was between 65–75 per cent. While one would be fairly confident in describing a person with such scores as 'of higher intelligence' than another who scored 40, 38, 43 and 44, one could hardly be confident of describing him as of higher intelligence than a person who scored 65, 69, 62, 64. [In practice one seldom has scores available for more than one occasion but it should be remembered that scores of psychological tests only indicate the rough placing on a scale in relation to other persons.]

Why do scores vary from one occasion to another? Well, human performance does actually vary from time to time. Anyone who plays tennis knows that he plays better on some days than others. There are some players near his own standard whom he would beat on some occasions and lose to on others. Other players well below his standard he would expect to beat even on his off days. Thus while human performance varies somewhat from day to day there is still a fair degree of consistency about it.

The second reason why test scores vary on different occasions is due to the nature of the test. The questions in most psychological tests are in multiple-choice form. This allows an element of guessing when the respondent is not certain of the right or most appropriate answer. In so far as there is a small 'chance' element in the score obtained this element is liable to vary from one occasion to the next.

12

The form of reliability indicated here (known as 'test-retest reliability) is measured by the *correlation* between the sets of scores obtained from the two separate occasions (see Appendix of this book and A8). Perfect reliability would of course give a correlation coefficient of unity ($r = 1.0$). The reliability of a ruler taking measures of the lengths of a series of lines may be about $r = 0.99$ with just the occasional variation as to whether the line is judged as 7.6cms or 7.7cms. Well-designed intelligence tests have reliabilities of the order of $r = 0.85$–0.90. Most personality tests and attitude scales have reliabilities below this ($r = 0.70$–0.90) (see D3).

Another common method of assessing reliability is by checking the correlations obtained between parts of the same test. This measure is perhaps better described as the internal consistency of the test. A great deal has been written about the concept of reliability in psychological testing and methods of measuring it. Those wishing to pursue the topic are advised to read Vernon (1960). The practical concern stemming from the reliability of a test is the probable error in scores obtained from the test. A small degree of error must be tolerated but if it becomes large the test will be of little value.

Validity
The second and more important characteristic of psychological tests is that of 'validity'. The validity of a test indicates how well it does the job it is designed to do. In the case of an intelligence test there is no 'true' measure of intelligence with which to compare test scores on one intelligence test to those of a second test. While one would be worried if the correlation was low, a high correlation does not necessarily indicate that either correlation does not necessarily indicate that either test is measuring 'intelligence'. It only indicates that they are both measuring

13

much the same thing.

Another approach is to compare the scores obtained on the test with behavioural outcomes that might be expected to be related to intelligence. For example, one would expect that success in an academic course of study would depend on the level of intelligence of the students. In fact the correlations obtained between well designed intelligence tests and success in academic courses are normally found to be positive, sometimes as high as $r = 0.60–0.80$. Correlations found between intelligence test scores and real life behaviour where intelligence might be thought to be demonstrated are usually positive but of a lower order. (Evidence of such validation studies are given in Chapter 5.)

The validity of a test of extraversion (see D3) may be measured by the relationship between the scores on the test and other indices of extraverted behaviour. Extraverts might be expected to talk more at a social gathering than introverts. If one surreptitiously timed the length of time each member of a social gathering spoke and on another occasion measured the degree of extraversion (e.g. on the Eysenck Personality Inventory, Eysenck and Eysenck, 1964), the correlation between the two sets of scores could be obtained. To obtain a reliable measure of the proportion of time people spend talking a relatively long session would be required or several sessions to iron out differences due to the topic being discussed. As far as the authors know this study has not been performed.

A small and hitherto unpublished study carried out by G. Jessup consisted of making judgements as to how fourteen people would score on the extraversion and neuroticism scales of the Eysenck Personality Inventory. Having done this he asked the sample to complete the test. This study took place over some weeks and not on one occasion. The subjects were all well-known to the author (colleagues at work, friends, wife, etc). The correlation obtained between actual scores and judged scores on the introversion-extraversion scale was $+0.82$ (with $N = 14$, $P > 01$) while that obtained on the neuroticism scale was $+0.28$ ($N = 14$, not significant).

The high correlation on the introversion-extraversion scale indicates the validity of the scale although it must be realized that the judge made these assessments with knowledge of the questions contained in the scale and was thus using these to define what he was looking for in the subjects. The relatively low correlation on the neuroticism scale may suggest a lack of validity of the scale but it might also be due to the author's inability to judge neuroticism. Certainly neuroticism is more difficult to perceive than extraversion which is essentially defined in terms of overt behaviour. Neuroticism (or the lack of it) as defined by the test items tends to relate more to fears, fantasies, thoughts and so on which are not directly observable.

The above study is only quoted to elaborate on the concept of validity. The number in the sample is of course very small and the 'probable error' in the correlations is thus quite high.

The reader will be realizing by now that the concept of validity as applied to psychological tests is far from simple. The validity of a test can only be expressed in relation to other variables. Thus a test may have many sorts of validity related to different external variables. A test should therefore really be described as valid or invalid for a particular purpose.

Discrimination

Psychological tests are about discrimination – sorting out individuals and placing them on a scale. The concept is fundamental to the design of tests, as test items (questions) must be chosen which effectively discriminate between individuals.

If a test was to consist of only one item which subject either got right or wrong, subjects would be divided into two categories (say 1 and 0). If a test has two items, subjects may fall into three categories (2, 1 or 0). Clearly to spread a group of subjects out along a scale covering at least 10–15 categories, tests must be designed to include a large number of items.

A further consideration is the difficulty of the item (in the case of aptitude tests) or more generally the *discriminant* power of the item in personality tests and attitude scales. If an item is too easy and all subjects get the right answer, they would all score 1 and be in the same category. This provides no information about the differences between people and is therefore of no value. Similarly if all the items in a test are relatively easy, say items where 80 per cent of the population get them correct and 20 per cent wrong, the test would tend to sort out the weakest subjects from the majority but would not usefully discriminate among the majority of subjects. To discriminate effectively throughout the entire range of the population to be tested, items should be carefully selected of varying difficulty level appropriate to that population.

Another reason why tests should be made up of a fairly large number of items is to provide an adequate sample of relevant behaviour. In order to test numerical aptitude it would be important to include a wide variety of numerical operations within the test rather than concentrate on one aspect (e.g. multiplication), as performance on this aspect may not be typical of the subjects' general level of performance. Tests are always attempts to measure important aspects of behaviour or a psychological attribute by presenting it as a standard set of questions. (It is a bit like taking real life behaviour into the laboratory to look at it under controlled conditions.) (see A1) Thus from a set of questions or scales which might be completed in, perhaps, thirty minutes, one attempts to draw general conclusions about an individual's normal manner of behaviour or feeling.

Designing psychological tests

Although this chapter has run through the important requirements and concepts in test design at a very simple level the actual process of achieving these objectives requires considerable technical skill, ingenuity and a fair degree of statistical sophistication. Test items must be created, tried out experimentally on large samples of subjects and the results analysed. Only items which discriminate effectively in terms of the characteristic being measured and which are of the appropriate level of difficulty are retained.

A test is normally designed in order to produce a 'normal' distribution of scores as shown in Fig. 1.1 for the population for which it is designed.

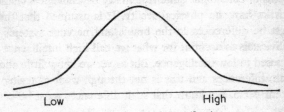

Low   High

Fig. 1.1 *The normal distribution*

The essential characteristic of this distribution is that few people score very high or very low and that the majority score in the middle ranges. The height of people is distributed in this manner, as are most physical characteristics and most psychological characteristics are believed to be similarly distributed. There are underlying genetic reasons for this phenomenon.

Hypothetical constructs

One very important distinction between the measurement of psychological characteristics as opposed to physical characteristics is that the former do not actually exist. That is to say they have no physical reality that we can point to. Concepts such as intelligence or achievement motivation are 'hypothetical constructs' (see A1) and can only be *inferred* from observable characteristics of individuals – that is their behaviour. Because psychological characteristics are 'hypothetical constructs' it is possible to use different sets of constructs to describe individuals. Eysenck (1960) for example uses two constructs (extraversion and neuroticism) to account for personality differences between individuals, whereas Cattell (1965) uses sixteen (see D3). The question is not whether Eysenck is right and Cattell wrong or vice versa. The relevant question is which form of description is most useful and most practicable in given situations. That is to say, which set of factors is best able to account for certain types of behaviour and predict future behaviour.

It is of course not quite true to say psychological characteristics have no physical reality. It is assumed that there must be differences in the brains and nervous systems of individuals to account for what we call high intelligence as opposed to low intelligence. But as yet we know little about such differences and this is not through want of trying in recent years. We know that such differences must be complex.

Many people are unhappy about using 'hypothetical constructs' to describe people because they are intangible. Although such constructs are convenient ways of thinking about people they are not essential for the practical purpose of predicting performance. It is possible to think in terms of performance in one situation predicting performance in another situation. Thus performance on a selection test may predict success in performing at a job some-

time later. Although psychological characteristics are difficult to define and can only be measured imprecisely they
nevertheless provide valuable insights into the behaviour
of people (including oneself) and provide useful information on which to base personnel decisions. This book will
illustrate their use in the context of work.

2
The assessment of intelligence and aptitudes

Intelligence and other specific aptitudes (numerical, mech
anical, musical, etc.) should be distinguished from the know
ledge and skills acquired by people during their life
Intelligence and aptitudes are more fundamental charac
teristics and relate to people's *potential* to acquire know
ledge and skills. The fact that I have no knowledge of th
Russian language does not necessarily mean I lack intelli
gence or linguistic aptitude as I have had no opportunity
to learn the language. My inability to cope with French
after years of study, on the other hand, does suggest my
linguistic aptitude is low or my intelligence is low, or both
As I have a fair degree of success in a number of othe
intellectual pursuits it would not appear to be my intelli
gence which is at fault; therefore we may conclude it i
my linguistic aptitude which is low.

Although intelligence and aptitudes are defined in term
of potential, given reasonable opportunity to acquire
knowledge and skills inferences about potential can be
made from people's ability to cope with certain sorts o
problem. This is the basis of most intelligence and aptitude
tests, although some tests attempt to assess basic reasonin

kills in a relatively pure form by using abstract figures. These have been particularly valuable in assessing the true potential of children who have been deprived environmentally.

There has been much argument as to the nature of intelligence and more generally, the structure of human abilities. That is to say, how abilities are related. Figure 2.1 shows the kind of results obtained when a group of school-children are tested on a wide range of tasks. Each cell shows the correlation between scores on one test with those on one of the others. Looking at these correlations, what is immediately obvious is that while some of them are around zero, none of them is clearly negative. Thus it appears that children who are good at multiplication are also good at addition, comprehension, spelling, handicrafts and swimming. The second thing that is clear is that some of these correlations are higher than others and that certain abilities cluster together more closely than others. The heavy lines in Fig. 2.1 show some of these clusters and we see that there is a cluster of numerical, a cluster of verbal and a cluster of motor abilities.

Theories of the relationships between abilities try to take account both of the fact that none of these correlations is clearly negative *and* of the fact that these observed clusters of high positive correlations occur. Some theorists have concentrated on the fact of all correlations being positive – eg. Galton in 1883 said

People lay too much stress on specialities thinking that because a man is devoted to some particular pursuit he could not succeed in anything else: they might as well say that because he has fallen in love with a brunette he could not have fallen in love with a blonde. It is as probable as not that the whole affair was due to general amorousness.

	vocabulary	spelling	comprehension	arithmetic problems	addition	division	memory span	chess	tennis	badminton
vocabulary		·7	·8	·2	·3	·3	·3	·1	·05	·05
spelling			·6	·3	·2	·2	·3	·2	·05	·05
comprehension				·2	·1	·1	·3	·2	·06	·05
arithmetic problems					·8	·8	·3	·3	·02	·02
addition						·9	·2	·2	·02	·02
division							·3	·15	·04	·02
memory span								·4	·04	·05
chess									·1	·06
tennis										·9
badminton										

Fig. 2.1 *Hypothetical example of the level of correlations obtained between tests given to a class of schoolchildren*

(Of course the sort of data in Fig. 2.1 was not available to Galton.) It was, however, just this kind of data which led Spearman in 1927 to develop a theory in which individual differences in performance were attributed almost entirely to variations in general ability, intelligence, or 'g' as he termed it, and to a much lesser extent to variations in abilities which were specific to each individual task. This theory does not explain the clusters of high positive correlations and Spearman would probably have modified it as the continued testing of schoolchildren yielded ever-closer approximation to the data of Fig. 2.1.

In contrast, Thurstone (1938) developed a theory which concentrated only on the clusters and ignored the overall positive correlations. Or at least he considered that the apparent general ability reflected in these correlations could be explained in terms of the overlap of specific families of abilities. He suggested that there are eight of these: perceptual ability, verbal, numerical and spatial ability, inductive and deductive reasoning ability, word fluency and memory. His theory has been much extended in recent years by the work of Guilford on intellectual abilities.

Burt's (1939) theory most accurately reflects the sort of data obtained by testing schoolchildren. He suggested that there is a general ability which predicts much of the variation in performance, but that there are also specific abilities: verbal, numerical and practical. His theory has been extended more recently by Vernon, whose thinking spans both intellectual and practical aptitudes.

The three original theories are compared in visual terms in Fig. 2.2.

Of the three most recent derivatives Vernon's (1961) is the most generally useful in that it covers a broader span of abilities than either of the others. Vernon sees abilities as being arranged in a hierarchy (see Fig. 2.3). First general ability, which predicts to some extent the amount of verbal or educational aptitude and the amount of practical and mechanical aptitude. Similarly the amount of verbal ability predicts to an extent the amount of creative or clerical ability – it does not however offer any prediction about the amount of spatial or mechanical ability.

Vernon's theory is not however directly based on empirical research in the same way as Guilford's. Guilford has concentrated upon mental abilities. As a result of administering a vast number of pencil and paper type tasks to large numbers of subjects, he claims to have isolated over

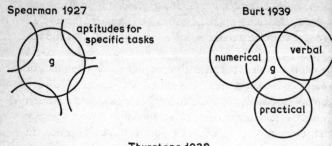

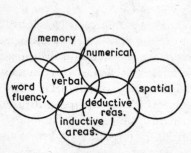

Fig. 2.2 *Three different ways of conceptualizing the structure of abilities*

a hundred different factors in ability. In his (1967) theory he isolates three dimensions of mental tasks: the content of the problem whether figural, symbolic, semantic or behavioural; the kind of operation which is performed e.g. understanding, remembering, convergent and divergent

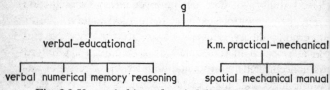

Fig. 2.3 *Vernon's hierarchy of abilities (adapted from Vernon, 1961)*

reasoning or evaluating and the product of this mental process e.g. an implication, a transformation, a single unit of information, a relationship and so on. This theory gives us a very different way of conceptualizing specific aptitudes. Instead of having an aptitude for dealing with verbal material it suggests we think instead in terms of an aptitude for carrying out deductive reasoning processes, using verbal material where implications are involved. This would be a different aptitude from that of evaluating the verbal implication. Sometimes it does seem important to differentiate aptitudes in this way: for example to differentiate between the convergent thinking required to pass examinations and the divergent thinking required for inventing new products. Often, however, it will be more useful to test for the existence of a broader range of aptitudes – most jobs demand an ability to perform a variety of operations on a variety of materials and yielding most of the different kinds of products.

Measuring intelligence
Early measures of ability were derived directly from tasks which people normally carry out. Thus the abilities of schoolchildren were tested through problems or activities which they were supposed to be learning in school anyway. As it became increasingly clear, however, that the ability to perform one task does predict to a greater or lesser extent the ability to perform others, tests of general ability, or intelligence, were increasingly sought. To begin with, in the days of Burt and Spearman, test items were selected or devised on the basis that 'everyone should have had an opportunity to learn how to do this'. If we look at the earliest test of general ability, that of Binet (which was first devised between 1905 and 1910 but extensively revised thereafter), we find such tests as being able to point to a paper cut-out doll's hair, eyes, mouth,

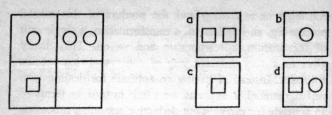

Fig. 2.4 *Raven's 'Matrices' type item – Complete the left-hand figure using one of the figures on the right*

feet and so on. This is for a two-year-old and the assumption is that all two-year-olds will have had the opportunity to learn such tasks. Similarly Burt's tests of general intelligence, which are for older subjects, rely heavily on such items as giving opposites, or completing a number series – things which it is assumed all children have the opportunity to learn at school. At this time the concept of general ability centred upon 'the ability to educe relationships'.

Later the concept of general ability returned to Binet's idea of learning ability and came to signify 'the ability to learn new principles and new relationships'. And the ability to learn was differentiated from what had already been learned. Good schooling and a stimulating environment became less important in determining scores on intelligence tests. Typical of these later tests is Raven's Matrices (first developed in the Second World War): an example of the kind of item involved is shown in Fig. 2.4. It is not obvious that any previous learning is necessary in order to solve this type of problem. However, research on institutionalized children suggests that certain kinds of experience are important; research connected with the old 11-plus examination that experience in doing similar tests helps; and cross-cultural research that not all societies instil the habit of carrying out meaningless tasks at high speed (see C4).

Despite the influences of environment, however, this test

has proved generally useful in assessing ability to carry out a very wide range of tasks. Thus it has been found to predict success in a variety of occupations such as nursing, engineering, the military and the police as well as success in university and college courses. Typically it does not predict such success very accurately: most correlations between test score and degree of success are in the region of $r = 0.3$ to 0.4.

More recent tests of general ability have also tended to make use of non-verbal items so as to minimize the influence of education on test scores. Cattell's 'Culture Fair' test (1963) is an example. Here picture series as in Fig. 2.5 are combined with matrix items and the test must be done at high speed. In Alice Heim's recent British test (1968; 1975), numerical and verbal problems form the first half of the test and a variety of non-verbal items follow. These recent tests incorporate two important innovations. First of all opportunity is given for the subject to learn how to solve the type of problems being set. Examples are given and the person administering the test ensures that everyone in the group understands the principles involved. This evens out initial differences in test sophistication. Second, different tests are used for groups which are expected to be of below average, average or superior levels of intelligence. (Cattell's test has all three versions and Alice Heim now publishes tests on four different levels. Raven's Matrices also now has three versions although the Advanced version is still in an experimental stage.) This has been found necessary in order to improve discrimination: on the Standard

Fig. 2.5 *Cattell's 'Culture Fair' type item – Complete the sequence on the left using one of the figures on the right*

version of Raven's, for example, a group of university graduates would probably all score between 50 and the maximum score of 60 and most of them between 55 and 60. If tested again, scores of the group would again fall mainly between 55 and 60 but each person's score would be slightly different. Discrimination would be impossible. At the other end of the continuum a group of mentally handicapped adults might all score between 0 and 10 on Standard Matrices and these scores would be equally useless for the purposes of discrimination.

Most methods of measuring general ability involve the use of pencil and paper exclusively and are designed so that a sizeable group can be tested simultaneously. This is not of course possible with young children: the original Binet test and its subsequent revised scales are administered in a one-to-one situation and most items do not require pencil and paper. They are either oral (e.g. repeating a list of digits, 375289), or else performance items (e.g. threading beads, building with cubes). There are also individual intelligence tests for adults, of which the best-known is the Wechsler–Bellevue. This contains both performance items and verbal/numerical/general knowledge items. Its advantage over group tests is that it is easier to motivate subjects in a one-to-one situation and it is also easier to get them to understand what is required of them. So an individual test can be particularly useful with subjects who are emotionally disturbed or who come from different cultures. It is not of much use in a conventional selection situation where a large number of applicants are being tested for a small number of jobs. It may be more appropriate where the potential of a particular individual is being assessed: whether in vocational counselling or in order to determine promotions or postings within an organization. Particular areas of strength and weakness can be more readily perceived in the one-to-one situation.

Measuring specific aptitudes

There are fewer tests of specific aptitudes than of general ability and they are of more recent origin; and there has been no general agreement as to what should be included within the range of specific aptitudes. Are specific aptitudes to be limited to Thurstone's primary mental abilities? Or to Vernon's abilities on the third and fourth levels? Or should the aptitude for any task be included?

In practice the range of aptitude tests includes any test which is predictive of success in a particular academic area, or in a particular occupation, or on a particular training course. They range from tests of artistic and musical aptitude, through the more intellectual aptitudes of verbal reasoning, spatial ability and creativity, to practical tests involving finger dexterity and hand-eye co-ordination.

Batteries of tests are available which either try to predict success in educational and training courses (e.g. Differential Aptitude Test – DAT) or in occupations (e.g. General Aptitude Test Battery – GATB). The Differential Aptitude Tests are pencil and paper tests resembling the group tests of intelligence. They cover verbal reasoning, numerical ability, abstract reasoning, spatial ability and mechanical reasoning, language usage and clerical speed and accuracy. Because they have been standardized mainly on American high-school students they can only show how like a particular individual is to an American student of, say Mathematics, or Modern Languages or Book-keeping. Some British norms are now becoming available, however, and the battery is useful in helping schoolchildren decide upon sixth-form subjects and upon what kind of vocational training to choose when leaving school. The results of the various tests are given as a kind of profile which shows up strong and weak points (see Fig. 2.6). One of its disadvantages is that all the tests are loaded with 'g' and that

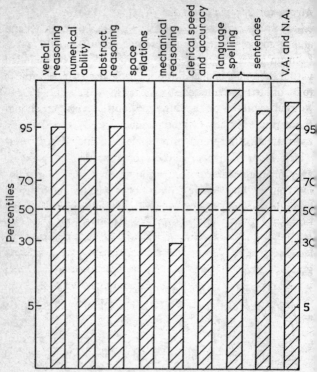

Fig. 2.6 *Example of Differential Aptitude Tests profile sheet (adapted from DAT, 1961)*

therefore people tend either to be good at everything or else good at nothing!

The General Aptitude Test Battery is linked more closely to occupations. It incorporates both pencil and paper tests (of computation, vocabulary, name and form matching, spatial ability etc) and tests of hand and finger dexterity. An individual's scores can then be compared with any of thirty-six occupational aptitude patterns which set minimum standards for acceptability in a range of occupations.

Again the norms are American, and it seems doubtful whether the same minimum standards would apply in this country.

In addition to the batteries of tests there are also individual tests available for specific aptitudes. And several of these do have British norms. The most widely used are probably those devised by the former National Institute of Industrial Psychology. These test a similar range of aptitudes to the DAT.

Predicting from present to future

How stable are abilities? Some theorists in the past have assumed that intelligence or general ability, at least, is inherited (see C1). It would therefore follow that provided we have once measured it reliably in an individual the level of general ability will not change as the individual grows older and there is no need to measure an individual's intelligence more than once. Present-day theorists, however, all agree that intelligence is affected both by heredity and by environment. They only argue as to which affects it more. On the one hand we have psychologists, like Jensen (1969) in America and Eysenck (1971) in England, who argue that approximately 80 per cent of the variance in intelligence within any particular group will be due to heredity and only 20 per cent to environment. On the other hand we have theorists like Vernon (1969) who argue that the percentages should be 60 and 40 per cent respectively. It is likely that neither is more than a rough guide. Where the environments of any two groups of people have been very diverse then there are always significant differences in their tested intelligence.

Children brought up in old-fashioned institutions where they are isolated from social contact and from the normal world typically have very low intelligence. They also typically improve greatly if their environment is altered (e.g.

31

Skeels and Dye 1939). Children brought up in complete isolation, as has sometimes happened, cannot attempt any kind of ordinary intelligence test. Yet they too can sometimes develop normally if their environment changes. On the other hand, if we take a group of children living in the same area with parents of the same socio-economic class and attending the same school then we are likely to find that differences in their levels of intelligence reflect differences in the intelligence of their parents. This area is one of considerable current controversy and it is not possible in the present chapter to develop the argument to any extent.

Specific aptitudes

There is less evidence concerning the inheritance of specific aptitudes. In general it appears that verbal and spatial ability are inherited to a greater extent than is numerical ability (Blewett 1954, Thurstone et al. 1953). Findings on reasoning ability are contradictory. With animals it is possible to control both heredity and environment more completely than with human beings. And animal studies show clearly that either may have an extreme effect on learning ability.

3
The assessment of personality

Personality is that which makes one person different from another and includes all the psychological characteristics of an individual. In this broad definition intelligence, aptitude and motivation would be subsumed under personality. More frequently in the psychological literature personality is used to describe the non-cognitive or non-intellectual characteristics of an individual. It refers more to the emotional make-up of a person and is reflected in the style of his behaviour rather than the quality of his performance (see D1). For the purposes of this chapter personality will be considered in this limited sense.

Because the area of personality is so complex and ill-defined theorists have approached it in a variety of ways (see D3). We cannot hope here to present any kind of an over-view of the different theories. We are confining the discussion therefore to a particular area in which the conclusions of different theorists are beginning to resemble one another and to those characteristics which have particular relevance to employment.

One basic source of individual differences in behaviour

is emerging in terms of the concept of introversion–extraversion (see D3). The concept has a long and varied history. Kretschmer, in 1948, observed a difference between mental patients who were classified as manic depressives and those classified as schizophrenics; the former tending to be short and fat and the latter tall and thin. He therefore suggested a constitutional difference which would not only predispose individuals to develop one or other of these mental illnesses but which would also determine differences in behaviour in a normal population. Thus the short, fat individual would be more affected by emotions and the tall, thin individual be more concerned with thought processes. Critics have argued that schizophrenia tends to develop in the late teens and early twenties whereas manic-depression develops in middle life, and that this age difference is sufficient to account for Kretschmer's observed differences. However, the distinction crops up independently in the work of Sheldon (1940). Using a normal university population Sheldon discovered that an individual's body build is closely related to the ratings which other people make of his behaviour. He isolated three basic types: the endomorph, fat and with an overdeveloped digestive system; the ectomorph, thin and with a highly-developed central nervous system; and the mesomorph, with large bones and well-developed muscles. The endomorph is rated as being sociable, relaxed and comfortloving, the ectomorph as being anxious and intellectual, the mesomorph as being aggressive and adventurous. The correlations are, if anything, too close to be credible.

It is unclear from this type of work whether the bodily configuration and the behaviour spring from the same underlying constitutional cause, whether the bodily configuration causes the behaviour directly, or whether behaviour leads to differences in body build. The first hypothesis is the most significant one, the second seems unlikely except in extreme examples, the third is both plausible and sufficient to explain Kretschmer and Sheldon's findings.

This basic distinction between the socio-emotive type and the thinking type had emerged in slightly different form in the writings of the psycho-analyst Jung. Jung based his theory of individual differences on introversion/extraversion. The introvert, for Jung, is someone who enjoys looking inward – at his own thoughts and feelings. The extravert on the other hand is an outward-looking individual who is mainly interested in people and events in the outside world.

In contemporary theory the distinction again emerges as a basic one. In the work of both Cattell (1965) in America and Eysenck (1960) in England introversion/extraversion has emerged as one of the two factors which account for the most variance in human behaviour. Both Cattell and Eysenck employ techniques of factor analysis (see F1) to discover what kinds of behaviour typically occur together in individuals. Thus by testing large groups it can be discovered that people who like going to parties also like jokes, enjoy physical activities, and are active and impulsive (i.e. are extravert types and like Sheldon's endomorphs and mesomorphs).

Beyond this basic similarity of technique Cattell and Eysenck have reached their conclusions about the importance of extraversion/introversion by different routes. Thus Cattell began with large quantities of different kinds of data-ratings of behaviour, answers to questionnaire items and performance on objective tests like pencil tapping or maze learning. From this data quite large numbers of factors (or clusters of related items) emerged (sixteen from the questionnaire data alone). However, some of these factors also themselves cluster together and yield second-order factors of which the two main ones are named

Anxiety and Exvia/Invia (which is intended to reflect its similarity to Jung's extraversion/introversion dichotomy).

Eysenck, on the other hand, has never concerned himself with more than the two factors of neuroticism and extraversion plus occasional reference to a factor of psychoticism (see D3). Eysenck's original concept of extraversion was borrowed from Jung and Sheldon but of recent years he has considerably modified it. The modifications stem from his experimental work in which groups of extreme extraverts (according to questionnaire data) are compared with extreme introverts on a variety of tasks. From such findings as the difficulty of conditioning extraverts, Eysenck developed the idea that extraverts set up cortical inhibition more quickly than introverts and disperse it more slowly.

The other main factor which emerges from current factor-analytic studies is Cattell's 'Anxiety' and Eysenck's 'Neuroticism' factor. (See Eysenck and Eysenck 1969: 239–53 for a demonstration of how this factor is common to the questionnaires of himself, Cattell and Guilford.) Here we find moodiness, anxiety, ill-health, feelings of guilt and inferiority clustering together to yield the neurotic type. Eysenck's views on the basis of neuroticism date from his work with hospitalized soldiers in the Second World War. He found marked differences in how strongly soldiers reacted to the stress of battle and the pain of injury. Those who reacted extremely to pain and stress he classified as 'neurotic' and considered that it reflected a constitutional characteristic of the autonomic nervous system (see A2).

Personality tests (see D3)

Instruments for measuring personality differ in two main ways:

a. Some are scored *objectively* (i.e. there can be no disagreements between different scorers) whereas others are scored *subjectively* (the scorer has to use his own discretion and judgement).

b. Some measure *verbal behaviour* while others use non-verbal *performance measures*.

Most of the measures of personality in current use have objective scoring methods. Both questionnaires and performance measures normally provide unambiguously scored data. Objectivity is, rightly, considered to be important in eliminating bias due to different scorers and in improving the reliability of the test.

There are still some personality measures, however, where the discretion of the scorer is important. These include projective measures (these are tests in which ambiguous or meaningless stimuli are presented and in which the subjects attempt to *project* meaning into such stimuli is considered to disclose important characteristics), and measures based upon observation of molar, large-scale aspects of behaviour.

Verbal projective measures – subjective scoring

Probably the most commonly used projective measures are the Rorschach and the Thematic Apperception Test. The Rorschach claims to measure a wide variety of personality dimensions including rigidity, ambition, insecurity, negativism, spontaneity, self-acceptance and intelligence by analysing the objects and scenes people perceive in ink-blot pictures like those shown in Fig. 3.1. Although the

Fig. 3.1 *Ink-blot diagram similar to those in the Rorschach test*

Rorschach manual gives guidance in how to 'score' the responses people make, it is inevitably the case that different scorers draw rather different conclusions about the same individual. For selection purposes therefore the test is of limited value – quite apart from the fact that it may take two hours or more to administer and score for one candidate.

The Thematic Apperception Test is concerned with motivation rather than personality and is discussed in chapter four.

Performance measures – subjective scoring
Assessing personality through the observation of behaviour is the oldest available method and is, of course, practised continually. The main way is by careful observation of present behaviour and by recalling past behaviours. In the selection situation we typically have records of past behaviour and these can often be a reliable guide to future behaviour in similar situations. We also, typically, have a sample of present behaviour in the interview. Many interviewers believe that it is possible to assess personality

characteristics from this sample of behaviour. In the past the assessment has tended to be based on an unanalysed 'general impression' but currently there are a few attempts to analyse the 'impression' into more objective components such as particular body posture, gestures and aspects of physical appearance. There is little evidence of the validity of such observations but some interesting relationships have been suggested: connections between high need to achieve (see D2 and D3) and a fast watch, flashy shoes and being culture-bound, tattoos and delinquency for example.

Verbal measures – objective scoring

Turning to genuinely objective techniques we find that these are mainly questionnaires or inventories. They thus measure verbal behaviour only, and of the self-report variety. Typical personality questionnaire items ask people to report on their likes and dislikes, their attitudes and what they would do in certain situations. It is therefore very easy to fake answers and to make oneself appear quite different if there seems to be a good reason for this. Would-be fakers should however note that they will be 'caught' by trick items. A recent guinea-pig succeeded in getting almost exactly the scores he was aiming for on the Eysenck Personality Inventory but simultaneously collected the maximum possible 'lie' score. William Whyte advises people that when faced with a personality test of any kind they should remind themselves that 'I loved my father and my mother, but my father a little more. I like things pretty much the way they are. I never worry about anything. I don't care for books or music much. I love my wife and children. I don't let them get in the way of company work.' He also suggests that personality tests prove valid in the selection situation because intelligent and highly-motivated candidates will work out what kind of people a particular organization is looking for and will complete

questionnaires as if they were that kind of person. Thu
the organization succeeds in recruiting highly intelliger
and well-motivated people!

In practice personality questionnaires are more generall
predictive of success at some occupations than at others
they are useful for salesmen and sales clerks, but not f
supervisors and foremen, nor for service workers (Ghisel
1973).

Different tests also vary in their usefulness but at th
point in time it is almost impossible to evaluate the ev
dence. The difficulty is due partly to the fact that tes
are often used without any check being made on the
validity; partly to the fact that the results of validatio
studies are seldom reported in journals, and partly to th
understandable reluctance of test devisers and distributo
to report negative findings. Moreover it is often the cas
that quite small differences in time and place will affe
validities. A test which distinguishes between successfu
and unsuccessful engineers in 1965 may cease to do so b
1970 and a test which picks out successful managers i
organization X may fail in organization Y, which has
rather different climate and style of operating.

In general a test which is ill-constructed or otherwis
unreliable cannot achieve validity. Many personality ques
tionnaires are doubtfully constructed, and Cattell's 16PF
often criticized on this basis. In fact it has probably attrac
ted more criticism than any other personality test whic
is in general use for selection, but this is partly because c
the extravagance of the claims made for it and partl
because it has been tried out in a variety of selection situa
tions for which it was not really appropriate. Other test
for which fewer claims are made, receive less attention
The Eysenck Personality Inventory, for example, is re
garded by Eysenck more as a research tool or a clinic
instrument than as a means of distinguishing the potenti

successes in employment from the potential failures. Nonetheless Lanyon (1972) states that 'there are many interesting correlates of extraversion and neuroticism in educational, industrial and clinical fields and the reported research in these areas continues to indicate general though not unequivocal support for Eysenck's theory of personality'. For example, Jessup and Jessup (1971) demonstrated that success in RAF pilot training was most likely for stable introverts and least likely for neurotic introverts (see Chapter 9).

The EPI is open to criticism on a number of points. For one thing it is short – only 57 questions. It thus takes only 10-15 minutes or so to complete and it does seem *a priori* unlikely that important differences in personality can be isolated in so short a time. However the length is comparable to that of other tests if it is remembered that Eysenck is concerned to measure two dimensions of personality only: extraversion and neuroticism. As the test is most commonly used it places an individual in one of four quadrants – see Fig. 3.2 – and differences in behaviour are predicted from this.

Many other questionnaires have been and still are being used for assessment and selection. Effective ones like the Guilford–Zimmerman or the Bernreuter usually turn out to be measuring the same two basic dimensions as the Cattell and Eysenck tests.

We are still far from being in a position to use personality questionnaires with any real confidence in either selection or vocational counselling situations. Cattell (1965) has pointed out that we need to know both about personality factors which determine adjustment in a job and those which determine efficiency, and he says:

even among those who stably stay in a job the two indices will rank people somewhat differently. For ex-

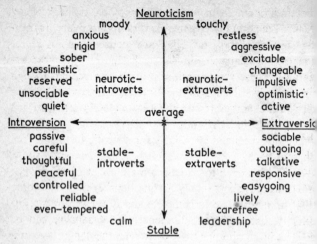

Fig. 3.2 *Eysenck's personality dimensions (adapted from Eysenck and Eysenck, 1964)*

ample scientific researchers are more 'premsic' than the general population. That is to say they are more emotionally sensitive ... But when correlations with a criterion of productivity and effectiveness such as patents gained researches published etc. are made in a group of researchers it turns out that premsia is negatively weighted. The ... tough and realistic scientist actually does a better job. (1965 : 348)

Performance measures – objective scoring
Objectively scored non-verbal measures of personality are still in their infancy. Cattell's (1965, 1967) work is again of central importance. He and his fellow-workers have devised a large number of highly ingenious tasks and have submitted scores on these to factor analysis in the same way as responses to questionnaire items. In these tasks 'the subject does not really know for certain in what way

his behaviour is being measured or what kinds of inference will be drawn from his test reactions' (Cattell and Warburton 1967).

Rather different personality factors emerge from the factor analysis of performance tests. However the main factors – of intelligence, extraversion and anxiety – which emerge from questionnaire data also emerge from the performance tests. Intelligence emerges in an independent but highly correlated form as 'harric-assertiveness' or 'fast, determined, effective action and self-expression' (Cattell and Warburton 1967). People who are high in this can keep up a fast speed of tapping, of reading and of swinging their arms; they see many objects in unstructured pictures and they spend a long time exploring a finger maze; they are also able to change quickly from one activity to another.

Extraversion reappears as 'exvia/invia' with the extravert also seeing many objects in an unstructured drawing, overestimating his own performance in a new task, preferring strange and dramatic stories to familiar ones and so on. These tasks may be compared with the tasks on which Eysenck finds differences between introverts and extraverts (as discriminated by his own questionnaire).

Anxiety also emerges from performance data; people high on this factor are easily annoyed, judge others' performance critically, get high marks at school, show large decrements in performance with noise and exert a low pressure when writing.

These measures have not yet been used much in selection or assessment situations. One major problem in their use is their unacceptability. They totally lack face validity. Thus both the individual candidate and the employing organization lack confidence in them. The candidate may not take the test seriously or may lose trust in the organization; the organization in its turn is likely to ignore the test

43

results. It is the opinion of the authors, however, that this type of test will eventually supersede questionnaires. A performance test, for example, is much harder to fake since it is nearly always impossible to know what is required. Moreover they usually call for actions which cannot be produced unless the candidate is capable of them. (For example one of the female author's more successful experiments in assessment demonstrated that highly-regarded police constables depress a morse key at a more even tempo than their less highly-regarded fellows.) If, as here, capacity is being measured then 'faking' is impossible.

4
The assessment of motivation

Motivation is related to personality but is orientated towards the goals people seek (see D2). Motivation is concerned with such questions as – What do people work for?
What do they enjoy doing? What leads to job satisfaction?
(see E5).

Table 4.1 Some goals people seek

1	2	3
food	money	a velvet dress
drink	friendship or social	a game of golf
warmth	interaction	pop records
oxygen	sense of achievement	cocktail parties
sleep	status or prestige	a sports car
avoidance of pain	security	books on Renaissance
	stimulation, interest	art
	or variety	a skiing holiday

Primary needs
People want, work for and enjoy a wide variety of things.
Everyone needs and will work for the goals in list 1. Most
people want most of the things in list 2 for most of the

time. Goals in list 3 are more individual: you may want two or three of them and positively dislike the rest. Theories of motivation seek to explain and predict these differences.

All theorists agree on the distinction between list 1 goals and the rest. Goals in list 1 are essential to the survival of the individual – a person who does not seek these goals will die. Often the theorist will add sex to the goals in list 1 on the basis that a species which does not seek to reproduce itself will die out. These are all physiological needs. They are innate and are common to all members of a species. (Physiological needs vary somewhat from species to species.)

Secondary needs

Early motivational theorists, like William James (1890) and McDougall (1923), considered that some of the needs in list 2 are also innate and common to all members of the human species: both suggested that gregariousness, sympathy, curiosity, parental love, combat or pugnacity are instinctive in this sense. Hull (1943) was the first to distinguish clearly between physiological (primary) needs and learned (secondary) needs. According to Hull each individual is born with primary needs. He then acquires secondary needs for those things which are, in his experience, linked to the satisfaction of these primary needs. Hull's own examples tend to be concerned with rat behaviour; thus the rat which is always fed in a white cage develops a need to be in a white cage and will show this by learning a maze to reach a white goal box or by crossing an electrified grid to reach it. Although Hull himself was concerned with rats the principle has been applied elsewhere. Cowles (1937) shows how chimps develop a need for poker chips or 'money'. The poker chips can be inserted in a 'Chimpomat' and out will come nuts and raisins. In order to get more poker chips the chimps will learn a variety of problems of perceptual discrimination. If the Chimpomat stops working the chimps continue to pile up the poker chips for a day or two, then stop. Once the machine is put right the chips regain their previous 'value'.

Likewise Winterbottom (1958) argues that the need for achievement is learned mainly as a result of parents' rewarding children for independent effort. Schachter (1959) suggests that the need for affiliation (friendship, social contact) is built up on the basis of how effective a child's mother is in satisfying his primary needs, in particular in helping him to avoid pain. If she is there to save him from danger and to soothe pain (as she tends to be more with her first-born than with later children) then the child learns to turn to people for help and comfort. Later-born children may turn to pills, alcohol, etc. Both Hull's original thesis and the developments of Winterbottom and of Schachter have been seriously criticized but they are unique in their capacity for predicting how and why individuals differ in their goals.

A need hierarchy

Maslow's (1970) theory of motivation (see D2) is less precise in its predictions. In Maslow's theory needs fall in a hierarchy as in Table 4.2. Physiological needs must be satisfied first but then the individual automatically develops a need for security. When this is satisfied to a reason-

Table 4.2 Maslow's need hierarchy

self actualisation: cognitive and aesthetic needs
↑
self-esteem
↑
belonging to a group
↑
security
↑
physiological needs

able extent he begins to need to establish relationships with individuals and to feel himself a member of a group. This satisfied, he develops a need for self-esteem and then finally he reaches the plane of self-actualization. On this level a man must be what he can be:

> it may loosely be described as the full use and exploration of talents, capacities, potentialities etc. Such people seem to be fulfilling themselves and to be doing the best they are capable of doing, reminding us of Nietzche's exhortation to become what thou art.

Maslow suggests that amongst other characteristics, self-actualizing people perceive reality more efficiently, accept themselves and others, are spontaneous and natural, focus on problems outside themselves, like solitude and privacy, are autonomous, open to experience, creative, humorous and have close interpersonal relationships.

Goals at work

Goals at work have usually been conceptualized rather differently, although Maslow's theory has been tested to some extent in work situations (e.g. Porter 1962, 1963; and Alderfer 1969) and attention has also been paid to the need for achievement in managers (McClelland 1961; Veroff *et al.* 1960).

Herzberg's two-factor theory

The most influential current theory of work motivation is probably that of Herzberg (1968) (see E1, E5). Herzberg distinguishes between aspects of a job which provide positive satisfaction for employees (motivators) and aspects which can only create dissatisfaction (hygiene factors).

He asks people – originally engineers and accountants of middle management levels – to think of a time when their job was particularly satisfying to them and to describe the aspects of the job that made it so. He found that such aspects as achievement, recognition, nature of the work itself, responsibility, advancement and personal growth are frequently mentioned in this context. When, on the other hand, people are asked to think of a time when their job was particularly dissatisfying and to isolate the incidents responsible, such aspects as company policy and administration, type of supervision and relationships with supervisors, work conditions and salary are mentioned most frequently (see Fig. 4.1).

Other researchers have had some difficulty in replicating Herzberg's findings. A common criticism (e.g. House and Wigdor, 1967) is that Herzberg's questions determine the kind of answers people give: thus it is socially acceptable to blame one's lack of job satisfaction on external conditions for which one is not responsible and equally acceptable to attribute one's sense of satisfaction to one's own hard work. Certainly these two dichotomous factors do not appear in research which adopts a different methodology. Another important criticism is concerned with interpretation. Some factors simply are more important overall than others. Many investigators (e.g. Armstrong 1971) find that the interest of the work itself is the main thing that determines both satisfaction and dissatisfaction. Herzberg's interpretation of his findings does rather mask the overall importance of the different factors; even in his own research the work itself contributes more to dissatisfaction than do salary, work conditions or relationships with other people at work. Really it is only company policy and type of supervision which can clearly be isolated as sources of dissatisfaction. Similarly personal growth contributes as much to dissatisfaction as to satisfaction.

Factors leading to dissatisfaction: Factors leading to satisfaction:
percentage of times mentioned   percentage of times mentioned

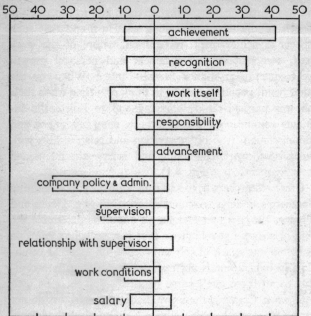

Fig. 4.1 *The main factors reported as creating job satisfaction /job dissatisfaction (adapted from Herzberg, 1968)*

Expectancy theory
The other main theory of work motivation may loosely be termed 'Expectancy Theory'. Its originator was Vroom (1964) and in its original form it simply stated:

a. that an individual works harder in a situation if he perceives that greater effort is likely to lead him to the attainment of goals which are important to him, and

b. that an individual is attracted more towards a job or work role which he expects will lead to goal attainment.

Porter and Lawler (1968) further elaborated the model by distinguishing between 'effort' and 'performance'. As may be seen from their formulation in Fig. 4.2 there is again no attempt made to predict the kind of goals that people have. It is assumed by each of the 'expectancy' theorists that individuals may have quite different goals. In order to predict how hard people will work or how well they will perform it is first necessary to know what their goals are. It is then necessary to know how they perceive the relationship between effort and goal attainment. If one wishes

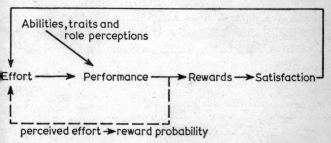

Fig. 4.2 *A performance-satisfaction model (adapted from Porter and Lawler, 1968)*

people to work harder it is necessary to somehow alter their perceptions of this relationship – or else to alter the relationship itself – so that they perceive increased effort as being likely to lead to satisfaction of needs.

Although this appears to be a commonsense view of human behaviour it has not proved easy to confirm through empirical studies. Georgopoulos *et al.* (1957) were able to show that high producers, amongst workers in a household appliance manufacturing company, were significantly more likely to have a high need for money, to perceive themselves as free to produce as much as they could, and to see high productivity as leading to their earning more money in the long run. But results for such goals as getting on well with the work group and for getting promoted were much less clear.

Measuring goals at work
Measuring motivation at work has thus traditionally been seen as a problem of measuring overall satisfaction with the work situation. This measure of satisfaction would then be correlated with output or performance, or perhaps related to different aspects of the work situation.

On the whole very simple measures of job satisfaction have proved to be as useful as the more sophisticated. The individual himself is as well able to weigh together the different factors involved as is the psychologist. Thus the 'fairly well satisfied' individual who puts his cross as shown

Fig. 4.3 *A scale of job satisfaction*

in Fig. 4.3 is reporting a feeling which is perhaps compounded of quite high satisfaction with some aspects of his job but quite low satisfaction with others. He can weigh the relative importance of these different factors better than any outsider could (see, for example Ewen 1967). This kind of overall measure of satisfaction is all that is required if we wish to compare satisfaction with output, or overall satisfaction before and after a change in working methods, or the overall satisfaction of workers in two different plants.

Motivation tests

Instruments for measuring motivation must first be divided according to whether they are concerned with assessing *individual differences in needs* or with assessing the *extent to which needs are satisfied.* They may also be divided according to the familiar distinctions between *objective* and *subjective scoring methods* and between *verbal* and *performance measures.*

Individual differences in needs (*verbal tests subjectively scored*)

It is convenient to begin with methods of assessing individual differences in motivation, of which there are few. The most important is the Thematic Apperception Test. This is a projective test with quite highly subjective scoring methods. It was first developed by Murray in 1943 and consists of a series of pictures about which the individual tells stories. He is asked to 'describe what has led up to the events shown in the picture, what is happening now, what the characters are thinking and feeling and what the outcome will be'. He will do this for twelve pictures. Certain 'themes' emerge in the stories – themes of achievement, affiliation, power, fear, aggression and so on. The number of times a particular theme occurs reflects the strength of that particular motive in the individual. It is assumed moreover that the individual will identify himself with the character in the picture who is most like himself in age and sex and that the thoughts, feelings and needs attributed to the character will reflect the individual's own thoughts, feelings and needs.

There is some experimental validation of this test in the work of McClelland and his associates. They first aroused certain needs in people, e.g. the need for achievement by giving an IQ test, the need for affiliation through a sociometric test which asked a group to name their best friends, the need for sex by having students rate the attractions of nude photographs, the need for escape by testing soldiers soon to be in the vicinity of a nuclear explosion. They were then able to demonstrate that the stories told about the pictures were different in predicted ways to the stories that were told before that particular need had been aroused (see Atkinson, 1958). As a measuring instrument the TAT is cumbersome, however. It takes at least an hour to test one individual; nor can it be shortened without losing its reliability and its capacity to test a variety of motives (though it may be possible to test a whole group at a time by exposing the pictures on a screen and having people write down their stories). Its other limitation is that its validity depends *absolutely* upon the co-operation of the individual being tested: and also upon the care, understanding and insight of the scorer. It is thus not a suitable instrument for selection purposes but might well be useful in the vocational counselling of certain clients. The motives which emerge, however, may not always be relevant to work situations.

Individual differences – verbal tests objectively scored
There are two remaining tests of individual motivation and these are both objectively scored.

One is the Allport–Vernon Study of Values which yields a profile showing the extent to which an individual is motivated by theoretical, economic, social, religious or aesthetic needs. Again the full co-operation of the individual is required. This is the test chosen by Whyte in *The Organization Man* to illustrate how very easily an intelligent candidate can deduce what the organization is looking for and emerge with a profile high on economic values, very low on aesthetic and fairly high on social and political (see Fig. 4.4). As he points out, the organization is usually wrong about its own needs but succeeds in this way in selecting highly intelligent people whose values are not primarily economic at all. Again the test could be useful in vocational counselling although it is not suitable for making selection or promotion decisions.

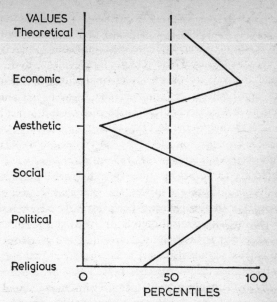

VALUES

Theoretical

Economic

Aesthetic

Social

Political

Religious

0   50   100

PERCENTILES

Fig. 4.4 *The Allport–Vernon study of values – suggested optimum executive profile (adapted from Whyte, 1963)*

Cattell's Motivation Analysis Test is also objectively scored and does in addition contain certain safeguards against faking. It is a more sophisticated instrument than the 16PF (see Ch. 3) and contains a variety of items, all of which, in some way, manage to conceal their true purpose. It is unfair to give examples of most types of items but one type is an item which appears as a test of information. Thus one might be asked to estimate how many people die of lung cancer in this country in a year. Very few people actually know the answer to this question and their estimate reflects their attitude and feelings rather than their knowledge. A high estimate would suggest a fear of developing lung cancer oneself.

The MAT test yields a profile of needs in the same way

as the Allport–Vernon. However the needs (or *sentiments* as Cattell describes them) covered vary more widely from career, through fear, assertiveness and mating to narcissism or comfort-loving. There is as yet little evidence to demonstrate the validity of the MAT in occupational settings although high career sentiment and high superego needs seem to bear a generally positive relationship to achievement according to the MAT Manual.

Individual differences – performance measures

These are all verbal measures of individual differences in motivation. There are in fact few performance measures. Persistence has sometimes been investigated by asking people to pick up small objects like nails and put them in a box which is then emptied and they are asked to pick the nails up again. Likewise it is considered that Raven's Matrices measures persistence as well as general reasoning ability; it certainly presents people with an equally meaningless task. Cattell has experimented a little with performance measures. He considers, for example, that the strength of any need could be measured by reading out material relevant to the satisfaction of that need while the subject(s) are being distracted by background noise. The amount heard and recalled would reflect the strength of that need. Any measure of amount learned and remembered would probably reflect the degree of interest in the material. Another possibility lies in such physiological measures of arousal as the psychogalvanic skin response (see A2). The psychogalvanic skin response measures the amount of perspiration on the fingertips (by electrical means) which is a symptom of stress or arousal. The response should be greater if an important need is aroused, whether by words or pictures.

As with performance measures of personality these tasks are not easy to use in assessment situations. It is hard to imagine the galvanic skin response becoming an acceptable way of selecting engineers or managers. Similar tests are, however, already used for selecting pilots and astronauts although in these cases it is simply a question of measuring reactions to general forms of stress rather than an investigation of specific needs. Again it is interesting to speculate as to whether the proven usefulness of Raven's Matrices as a selection instrument is due to the fact that it measures ability or to the fact that it measures persistence.

5
The assessment of attitudes

Mr A grew up in the Depression of the thirties. His father was a coal-miner and frequently out of work. Now Mr A is a trade union leader. How does he feel about the National Coal Board? does he have a high or low opinion of management? How does he behave during negotiations?

Mr X is a newly-promoted thirty-year-old black foreman. Mr Y is a semi-skilled shop floor worker of fifty-one. How is Mr Y likely to feel about Mr X? What does he think of him? How will he behave towards him?

Both Mr X and Mr A have Attitudes (see B1, B3). One can have attitudes towards individual people, towards identifiable groups of people, towards ideologies, towards things. An attitude implies that one will think in a certain way, feel in a certain way and be predisposed to act in a certain way towards the objects of one's attitude. In practical terms, the predisposition to act in a certain way is clearly the most important component (Doob 1947). Often, however, the only way we can infer such a predisposition is by measuring thoughts and feelings (since the behaviour itself has not yet occurred). Sometimes, too, people's behaviour is inconsistent with their thoughts and feelings: indeed they even behave in a different way to the way they expect themselves to behave. In a classic study of racial prejudice, for example, La Piere (1934) travelled around America with a Chinese couple. They stopped at 66 hotels and 184 restaurants and were refused service once. Six months later La Piere wrote to all these establishments asking if they would serve Chinese guests. Only about half replied, but of these 92 per cent said they would not serve Chinese. Behaviour differs from thoughts and feelings and expectations because of the presence of additional social pressures: in this case the receptionists probably wanted to avoid embarrassment; often people inhibit their behaviour out of a realistic fear of the consequences. The thoughts and feelings remain important however, because, if the inhibition is removed, then the appropriate behaviour will occur. We can observe this happening in many crowd situations, in gang warfare and in trades union negotiations.

When we attempt to measure attitudes we are therefore concerned with cognitive, affective (emotional) and behavioural components. Most attitude scales that we use will contain items concerned with each of these.

Measuring the cognitive component

Let us suppose that we are trying to measure workers' attitudes towards a particular organization. On the cognitive side we might first ask 'what words or concepts do workers use in describing an organization? How do they differentiate between bad and good organizations?' This might well lead us into the use of a modified version of Kelly's (1955) Repertory Grid (see F1). We might prepare a series of cards each having the name of a well-known organization or type of industry on it. People would then be presented with three cards at a time and would be asked to group two of them as being alike and different from the third. For example, they might group 'ICI' and 'car factories' together, differentiating them from 'textiles' because they are thought to pay higher wages. They would then verbalize the distinction they had made and state which is 'bad' and which 'good'. In this simple way we could discover the concepts that people actually use in judging organizations, and, by taking the Repertory Grid technique one stage further, we could determine more precisely how many concepts are used and how important each one is. It is probable, however, that, as Triandis (1959) found, there are wide individual and group differences in the concepts used and that managers, clerks and shop floor workers in particular regard different things as being important.

Having discovered the concepts which seem to be important to people, these concepts may be arranged in a form of an Osgood et al. (1957) Semantic Differential scale (see B1 and B3), like this:

large	├─┼─┼─┼─┼─┤	small
friendly	├─┼─┼─┼─┼─┤	unfriendly
pays well	├─┼─┼─┼─┼─┤	pays badly
dirty work	├─┼─┼─┼─┼─┤	clean work
expanding	├─┼─┼─┼─┼─┤	doing badly

Since we already know which end of each scale is 'good' or 'bad' we can use the scale for measuring how favourable workers' attitudes are to any given organization.

Still on the cognitive side we might examine people's beliefs about the organization. Hammond (1948) used a technique similar to that of Cattell in the MAT in that he presented workers with this kind of choice:

| What percentage of workers' salaries is made up of fringe benefits? | 90.60.40.10 |

Given that the true percentage is 50, a choice of 90 or 60 indicate a positive attitude, a choice of 10 or 40 a negative attitude. Similarly, if asked

How much does the Managing Director earn?	£70,000, £50,000 £30,000, £10,000

it might be that only the choice of £70,000 indicates a negative attitude. As with the MAT, the subject is unaware that his attitudes are being measured.

A third and final approach along cognitive lines was evolved by Triandis and his associates (Triandis 1971). In this approach he looks for the antecedents and consequences of certain organizational characteristics. For example workers might be asked:

If you have a large organization then you have:

better pay:
    probable ├───────┼───────┼───────┤ improbable
greater job security
    probable ├───────┼───────┼───────┤ improbable
a more friendly supervisor
    probable ├───────┼───────┼───────┤ improbable

This kind of measure could be particularly useful in assessing attitudes towards specific organizational changes. It could give advance warning of widespread unfavourable attitudes towards a proposed change and also indicate which departments or groups are particularly unhappy about it.

Measuring the affective component

Measuring the affective component of attitude has traditionally attracted the bulk of research effort. The most direct way of measuring degree of affect is to use physiological measuring instruments. Thus the extent to which the fingertips sweat (the psychogalvanic skin response) when a particular stimulus is presented indicates the degree of emotional arousal created by that stimulus. Similarly the extent to which the pupil of the eye dilates is also an index of arousal (see A2). These measures are not without their attendant difficulties however. They are in the first place extremely volatile measures: both the galvanic skin response and pupil dilation are sensitive to so many stimuli in the internal and external environments that the response to a presented stimulus is hard to measure with any accuracy. There is no clear 'base-line' from which to measure changes. The measures obtained also seem to vary greatly from one occasion to another. Secondly it is difficult to present many of the stimuli in which we are interested – how can stimuli like organizations, unions, pay etc. be meaningfully and unambiguously presented? Thirdly it is usually an impracticable procedure since it involves very considerable amounts of time being set aside for it. Finally, and most disturbing, there is no way of knowing whether the emotional arousal is favourable or unfavourable in the case of the galvanic skin response and the distinction is not at all clear in the case of pupil dilation either.

Verbal methods of assessing the affective component of attitude have therefore been used more often. All verbal methods begin in a similar way by collecting a variety of statements about (in this case) the organization. 'This organization is like a big happy family', 'This organization has a lot of lazy workers in it', 'Most of the machine tools here need replacing' and so on. The attitude assessor may make them up himself, he may ask his colleagues for help or, better still, he may collect the views of people who work in the organization. In deciding which of the statements to use and how exactly to get people to respond to them he is likely to employ one of three techniques, each of which is outlined below. Behind each of the techniques lies the assumption that the assessor should not allow *his* attitude to be apparent. Therefore an equal number of statements should reflect positive and negative attitudes. It is not easy to determine *a priori* just how positive or negative a particular statement is and the three techniques are simply ways of determining this.

Thurstone (1928) evolved a method whereby a number of judges placed each statement in one of eleven piles according to how favourable they thought it was. Thus a particular judge might place 'this organization is like a big happy family' in pile eleven to indicate maximum favourability and 'most of the machine tools need replacing' in pile three to indicate definite but not maximum unfavourability. He might reserve pile one for such statements as 'the firm is going bankrupt' and 'top management is totally incompetent'. Thurstone retained only those statements which got the same, or similar, rankings from most people. Amongst the statements which remained he then chose a series which proceeded in equal steps from the most to the least favourable. These statements would be arranged in order and people would indicate whether or not they agreed with each one.

Table 5.1 shows five items from a Thurstone attitude scale developed by Uhrbrock (1961):

Table 5.1

Statement	Average scale value
If I had to do it over again I'd still work for this company	9·5
The wage incentive plan offers a just reward for the faster worker	7·9
I believe accidents will happen no matter what you do about them	5·4
My boss gives all the breaks to his lodge or church friends	2·9
An honest man fails in this company	0·8

Uhrbrock's extensive list of statements about work situations together with their scale values has been widely used for developing attitude scales of the Thurstone type. However, after fourteen years some of the phraseology is out of date and the scale values may not be reliable. In general the Thurstone scale is found to be not quite so reliable as the two following methods (Poppleton and Pilkington 1964; Tittle and Hill 1962).

It is currently more common to use a Likert (1932) type of attitude scale. A Likert scale does not require the prior work of determining scale values and developing a scale with equal-appearing intervals. A series of statements is collected as before, reflecting both positive and negative attitudes. A number of subjects then respond to the statements by a. strongly agree, b. agree, c. uncertain, d. disagree, e. strongly disagree. The assessor will already have decided *a priori* which statements reflect positive and which negative attitudes. He can therefore pick out a group of the subjects who are clearly positive and a group who are clearly negative in their attitudes. The responses of these two extreme groups to each of the statements are compared. Only those statements are retained to which the positive group respond positively and the negative group negatively. The scale may then be administered although further item analysis (see p. 17) should be carried out to ensure that all the statements correlate as predicted with the total score.

The Likert type of scale is preferred because it is easier to devise and also because people prefer the greater freedom of response it offers. People seldom simply 'agree' or 'disagree' with a particular statement. Usually they want to be able to express their reservations and sometimes they are quite unable to decide whether they agree or not.

Guttman's (1944) scalogram analysis is very much a combination of the previous two methods. Guttman usually uses a Likert-type scale but seeks to place the statements in logical order so that an individual who agrees with the first statement and disagrees with the second will necessarily disagree with all the rest. An example of hypothetical responses to the favourable end of such a scale is shown in Table 5.2. In most areas they are extremely difficult to devise since attitudes are complex and people somewhat illogical. When they can be devised they have the advantage that the assessor can be confident that he is measuring just one attitude and not a combination. This may be very important if organizational change is to be based on the results of his measures.

Table 5.2

Statement	Response of individual			
If I had to do it over again:	A	B	C	D
I'd still work for this company	Yes	No	No	No
This organization is like a big happy family	Yes	Yes	No	No
Managers here consult with the workers	Yes	Yes	Yes	No

Most of these attitude measures we have discussed demand quite a high level of reading ability plus the ability to reason with words. However investigators are often interested in the attitudes of people who are not very good with words.

If time is unimportant in a particular situation then attitudes can be investigated in individual interviews. It is easier for people to answer questions orally than it is for them to understand the written word and also the interviewer can rephrase any questions which are not easily understood.

If time is a problem, then measures like the Job Descriptive Index (Smith, Kendall and Hulin 1969) can be used. Here the worker merely circles Yes, No or ? to indicate whether or not certain adjectives describe his present job.

To make it clearer whether or not these factors are important to him he may also be asked about his previous best and worst jobs, thus:

Best job		Present job		Worst job	
routine	Yes ? (No)	routine	Yes ? (No)	routine	(Yes) ? N
hot	(Yes) ? No	hot	(Yes) ? No	hot	(Yes) ? N
challenging	(Yes) ? No	challenging	Yes ? (No)	challenging	Yes ? (N

With this additional information we can infer that the particular worker who answered as above likes his present job in that it is not routine and he does not mind the heat, but he dislikes his present job in that it is not challenging.

Using this kind of technique and applying factor-analysis to the obtained results it usually appears that there are five factors involved in the total sense of satisfaction. These are:

1. satisfaction with the nature of the work itself (we have already noted the importance of this factor when discussing Herzberg's theory);
2. satisfaction with pay;
3. satisfaction with promotional opportunities;
4. satisfaction with supervisors and the type of supervision;
5. satisfactory relationships with co-workers.

Measuring the behavioural component

The behavioural component of attitudes has been approached in two quite distinct ways. Bogardus and Triandis have approached it in terms of intended behaviour. This is not in fact a way of measuring behaviour at all but falls somewhere between a statement of affect and the actual behaviour which may follow:

Statement of affect	Statement of intended behaviour	Behaviour
I dislike this organization and would like to resign	I shall hand in my resignation later this year	handing in of resignation

Most attitude scales will include 'intended behaviour' items because they are easy to understand and identify with. The most positive attitude towards an organization is reflected in the behaviour of joining it just as the most unfavourable is reflected in the behaviour of leaving it. Even more clearly, favourable attitudes towards people are reflected in being willing to accept the person as a close friend or as a marital partner, negative attitudes in being unwilling to live in the same neighbourhood (Bogardus 1931).

Measurements of actual behaviour should be even better indicators of attitudes. But are they? Does the number of students at a lecture reflect a, the quality of the lecture; b, the time of day/day of the week; c, the extent to which examination questions are based on lecture material; d, whether or not the lecturer keeps a register of attendance? Behaviour is a combination of norms, habits, and reinforcement schedules (see A3) as well as the cognitive and affective components of attitudes.

Campbell (1950) and Webb, Campbell *et al.* (1966) have been active in the search for behavioural indicators of attitudes. Their ingenious suggestions range from assessing the value of a picture in a gallery through the degree of wear which the floor in front of it receives to doll-play techniques (long used by child psychotherapists) to reveal attitudes of liking and disliking towards groups and individuals.

These behavioural indices are particularly useful in

situations where people are likely to wish to conceal their true attitudes. Where no such motivation is present, however, it is possible to obtain a more sensitive assessment by the use of verbal attitude scales which allow quite subtle variations in attitude to emerge.

In practice behavioural indicators are used quite widely in the employment field, where it seems to be accepted that leaving your job means that you did not like it, and that frequent absences and low productivity also indicate low morale. But again these tend to be somewhat gross measures which allow the general level of morale to be assessed but not the causes of it. They are of little use in the management of organizational change except insofar as they indicate that some kind of change is desirable.

6
The assessment of performance

Why assess performance? Clearly in order to facilitate the making of certain decisions: whether to promote, demote, discharge, transfer or retrain an individual and whether to give him merit pay increases in some organizations. More subtly, perhaps, in order to motivate employees to work harder and to persuade managers to give more careful thought to the capacities and potentialities of their subordinates.

Before we can assess performance in a job we must know what the job is. We must know what tasks are carried out and what the individual's responsibilities are. We must also know the criteria for successful performance and whether some parts of the job are more important than others. There is no simple fool-proof way of doing this. The best way of drawing up a job description remains that of asking the worker what he does and how much time he spends on each component of the job. This description may then be checked with the immediate superior and precise responsibilities agreed between them. This procedure is likely to be more accurate than one which relies on the testimony of the worker or manager alone.

In the case of a secretary we might arrive at the following analysis, which would lead to a simple assessment of how well each function was performed:

Duties – main	Percentage of time	How well performed
1. Take dictation and type up letters, memos and reports	40	
2. Maintain filing system	10	
3. Answer routine telephone enquiries, putting non-routine calls through to boss	20	
4. Obtain and send out certain kinds of information in response to certain routine enquiries	15	
5. Receive visitors	10	
Duties – occasional		
6. Make bookings and arrange travel	5	
7. Act as 'hostess' at office functions		

The problem with this type of performance assessment is that it does not allow us to compare one employee with another unless they are performing precisely similar jobs. And in most organizations this will defeat the purpose of facilitating decisions on promotion and transfers. It enables us to look only at how a particular individual performs a particular set of tasks. In order to compare one individual with another all must be assessed on the same dimensions. There are many ways of doing this.

Ranking

Ranking is the simplest technique of all. Each manager or supervisor ranks the people under him according to certain dimensions – output, quality of work, value of the organization etc. He will first select his most outstanding subordinate, then his worst, and will then place others in rank order between the two. The method has the advantage of forcing the manager to discriminate between people: he cannot assess more than one person as 'average' nor can he group the majority together in a 'somewhat above average' position. At the same time it is unlikely that all the discriminations he makes are meaningful and reliable – particularly if he has a group of more than twelve to twenty people working under him. There is also the difficulty of comparing people who have been ranked by one manager with people who have been ranked by another. It may be that all the subordinates of manager A are superior to all the subordinates of manager B: it is certainly unlikely that they are of precisely similar calibre.

A variant of the ranking technique is to present the manager with a series of randomly arranged pairs of his subordinates. He then chooses the better from each pair. Normally all the possible combinations of subordinates would be presented but this soon becomes very large (if he has twelve subordinates then sixty-six pairs are required but for twenty subordinates the number rises to 190). Rambo (1959) has suggested that only half the possible combinations need be presented, but taking into account the length of time to score responses it seems unlikely that the technique of paired comparisons has any great advantage over simple ranking procedures.

Forced distribution
The technique of forced distribution takes into account the fact that, in ranking, the difference between an outstanding subordinate and his nearest rival is greater than the differences between subordinates who are near the average. It implies a normal distribution curve and demands that the manager assigns a small percentage of subordinates extreme grades and a large percentage intermediate grades, as shown below in Figure 6.1.

If the subordinates are, in fact, normally distributed for performance then this technique is helpful. Unfortunately, unless there are very large numbers of them, this is most unlikely. Any particular manager is likely to have a pre-

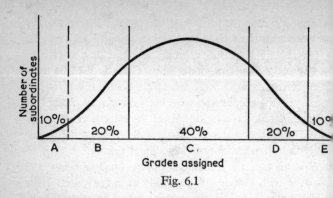

Fig. 6.1

ponderance of above- or below-average subordinates if compared with the organization as a whole. Again, then, it is impossible to compare one manager's subordinates with those of another.

Rating scales

In the effort to ensure comparability rating scales are often introduced. These will be similar to the rating scales discussed in Chapter 5. Some examples are given in Figure 6.2. The same two subordinates 'p' and 'q' have been ranked on each scale.

The most important variations are in (a) the number of points on the scale and whether this is an odd or even number and (b) whether or not verbal descriptions are given for typical behaviour at each point on the scale.

First the number of points on the scale. If we look at the assessments of subordinate 'p' we can see that only his markings on scale *b.* are out of line. With only three points on the scale very little discrimination can be made. If we look at subordinate 'q', however, we see that there are differences in assessment depending upon whether there are an odd or an even number of points on the scale. Given an even number as in scale *c.*, this subordinate is

a. Motivation

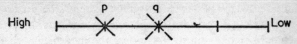

High   p   q   Low

b. Motivation

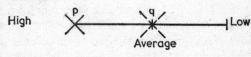

High   p   q   Low

Average

c. Motivation

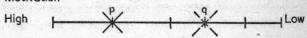

High   p   q   Low

d. Motivation

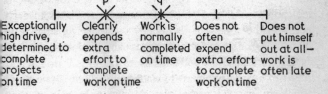

| Exceptionally high drive, determined to complete projects on time | Clearly expends extra effort to complete work on time | Work is normally completed on time | Does not often expend extra effort to complete work on time | Does not put himself out at all— work is often late |

e. Motivation

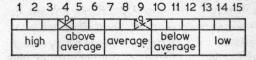

| 1 | 2 | 3 | 4 | 5 | 6 | 7 | 8 | 9 | 10 | 11 | 12 | 13 | 14 | 15 |

| high | above average | average | below average | low |

Fig. 6.2 *Rating scales*

73

pushed to a below-average rating. Similarly in *e*. the finer distinction called for after denoting him 'average' reveals the fact that he is only just average. It might be deduced from this that the ideal scale is long and has an even number of points on it. But in fact the more points there are the more difficult rating becomes and the differences quickly become meaningless. The fifteen-point scale in *e*. would be too difficult if it were not first broken down into a simpler five-point scale. In general it is thought that raters are only able to use a five- to seven-point scale meaningfully.

Secondly there is the question of giving verbal descriptions. Anstey (1961) suggests that whether or not verbal descriptions are given should depend upon the number of people a manager typically reports on. Where a manager is reporting on a large number then he can easily use a scale (giving the top 10 per cent of workers the top marking and so on). But when he is reporting on only one or two people doing a similar job the verbal descriptions are important in indicating what kind of performance corresponds to each point on the scale. He also points out, however, that 'it is by no means easy to frame five clear and distinct statements against each heading' and sometimes 'definitions do not add much to a simple request to classify people on a five point scale'. In general verbal descriptions only help if they indicate specific kinds of *behaviour* on the part of the subordinate.

There are also problems inherent in any scale. These problems stem from basic difficulties in assessing and rating other people. Thus the 'halo effect' tends to occur: if a manager has just given an 'above average' rating for a quality he considers important, e.g. output, he is then likely to give the same subordinate 'above average' ratings for other qualities too. Then there is also a tendency to rate leniently: whatever a particular scale measures there is a tendency to use the 'above average but not outstandingly good' categories most often, see Table 6.1.

Table 6.1 Distribution, in percentages, of grades awarded for job performance in six firms

Out-standing	More than adequate	Adequate	Barely Adequate	Poor	Unproved
7	42	44·6	2·6	0·2	3·6

(Adapted from Rowe 1964)

And going along with the leniency effect is a 'central tendency' whereby raters use the 'average' category when they are unsure about what rating to give. All these tendencies reduce the usefulness of rating scales although if they are understood their effects can be reduced considerably – either through careful design of the scale's format or through differential weighting of different points on the scale.

Forced-choice ratings
The forced choice technique was introduced by Sisson (1948) specifically to counteract the leniency trend. In its original form raters have to choose which of two equally favourable statements applies most closely to a subordinate. Careful prior research establishes statements of equal favourability but of which only one is relevant to success on the job. For example, secretary 'always arrives on time' might be paired with 'is exceptionally well-dressed', and 'does not keep her office tidy' might be paired with 'does not maintain the filing system efficiently'.

A number of other versions of the forced-choice method have been tried out, and Berkshire and Highland (1953) have concluded that the form which reduces leniency and halo effects best, whilst remaining popular with raters, is a form in which fair statements about the subordinate are presented and the rater chooses the two which describe the subordinate best. A good deal of work is involved in developing this kind of rating scale but it is easy for managers to use (which cuts down training time) and is also easy for the personnel department to score. It is also possible to build into such a scale specific measures of breadth of capacity, flexibility and other qualities particularly relevant to questions of transfer and promotion.

Critical incidents technique
The final method of assessment we shall examine is the critical incidents technique introduced by Flanagan (1949). Interviews with supervisors and managers are used to establish events which indicate particularly effective or ineffective performance in specific jobs. Depending upon the type and level of job these incidents can vary from 'using the wrong size bolt' to 'failing to get prior approval of an interested party' or from 'detecting a worn machine part before breakdown occurred' to 'discovering a computer programming error before figures were distributed'. From these examples it can be seen that critical incidents tend to be specific to particular jobs. Broad categories of types of error, or of types of good performance, do emerge, but are not strictly comparable across grades or types of job. The procedure is also extremely time-consuming: in Flanagan and Burns' (1955) application of the technique to foremen in Delco-Remy, for example, the foremen considered that they would have to keep daily records of the incidents as they occurred. Its great advantage seems to lie less in assessment than in staff development. A record of an individual's effective and ineffective actions can be extremely useful both for day-to-day coaching purposes and also for the yearly or half-yearly appraisal interviews he is likely to have with his manager.

Conclusion

There are certain general points which have emerged from our discussion of particular techniques of assessment. Whatever technique is adopted it seems that the following should be borne in mind:

1 It is important to establish the purpose of the ratings. Is it essential to be able to compare individuals from different departments or is it for the sole purpose of merit increases and individual development?

2 It is important to understand the raters: they are usually unwilling to give unfavourable ratings; they find it hard to assess people on general traits which are not tied down to specific behaviours; unless carefully trained they are likely to 'bunch' their ratings around the average. They are also prone to prejudice, projection and a host of other defence mechanisms which prevent them from assessing others accurately. They therefore need careful training and also need to discuss their assessment with colleagues on a continuing basis.

3 No assessment technique can guarantee reliable and accurate reports. On the whole the simpler the ratings demanded and the more closely they are tied down to specific behaviours the more accurate they are likely to be.

7
The interview as a method of assessment

Types of interview

Interviews may be carried out in a one-to-one situation; or a group of interviewers may interview a single candidate; or a single interviewer may interview a group of candidates. Each type of interview has its advantages and disadvantages.

The one-to-one interview is the most common. It has the advantage of being the most natural situation. It is easier to build up a relationship with the candidate; he will feel at ease and will answer questions more fully and more naturally. In this way the interviewer is likely to find out a good deal about the candidate. In particular he will be in a good position to find out whether or not he would want the candidate to work with him or under him. These advantages carry with them certain disadvantages. The interviewer may be so strongly affected by his own positive or negative feelings that he is unable to assess the candidate fairly. The interview may be so relaxed that the interviewer 'forgets' to explore certain areas: it may turn

78

into a conversation about topics of mutual interest. The candidate himself or the interviewer's organization are likely to feel that the procedure is somewhat unfair; a prospective employee ought not to be accepted or rejected on the basis of an interview with just one person. And of course unless the interviewer is highly skilled the candidate and the organization are right – because the best people are not necessarily going to be selected. The procedure might then be altered to include additional one-to-one interviews.

The next most common type of interview is the Board interview. This is usually adopted by larger bureaucratic organizations in order that the selection procedure shall be seen to be fairer to candidates and so that people who are selected reach some kind of common standard. It also has some other advantages. A Board may be more conscientious in covering all relevant areas simply because members keep a critical eye on one another. They may also be more careful in reaching a decision based on all the available evidence. Often the questioning in a Board interview is crisper and more relevant – partly because of the critical presence of other Board members and partly because when any particular Board member loses inspiration another can take over. Also an inexperienced member can learn from others about questions to ask and the standards to use. There are also attendant disadvantages. The procedure tends to be very formal and the candidate will not be able to forget that he is being assessed. This makes him cautious and self-conscious – he does not behave entirely naturally. If each interviewer is given a topic and has only a short predetermined time allowed him it will often happen that he has to drop a subject just as it becomes interesting; the candidate suffers similarly from the effects of constantly changing people and subject matter. If, alternatively, the Board operates a more flexible system some candidates will have to face a stressful barrage of questions from all sides.

Although the Board may make use of more evidence in making their decision and the bias of individuals may be diluted, the group decision-process also has difficulties. Sometimes the chairman may use his position-power and override other members. Sometimes members will make irresponsible decisions based on too high a degree of risk-taking. This is a common phenomenon in small decision-making groups (see, for example, the excellent review by Dion, Baron and Miller 1970) and seems to be the result of no one member carrying ultimate responsibility for a group decision (see B2).

The third type of interview is less common. As it is usually run it is less of an interview and more of an observational technique. Typically a small group of candidates (about six to twelve) will sit around a table or in a circle and their behaviour will be observed by one or two 'interviewers'. The interviewers do not normally interact with the candidates except to give instructions. The group may be given a series of topics to discuss or they may have problems to solve. The observers are then able to assess the quality of the contribution made by each member.

Advantages of this kind of 'interview' are:

1 group members usually become very involved in the tasks set and therefore behave fairly naturally;

2 because the interviewer is not involved he can observe behaviour more accurately – although he has more people to observe;

3 it gives an opportunity to judge how well the candidates are likely to get on with their colleagues and how well they work in a team, how good they are likely to be at running meetings, and how influential they are likely to be.

The attendant disadvantages are that the nature of other group members may affect a particular individual either positively or negatively: if other members are passive then it is easy to influence them; if the individual dislikes all other members he may be unwilling to interact with them at all; if a group has one very aggressive, dominant or otherwise difficult member, others may give up trying to work in that group. In these cases the interviewers do not see the individual behaving either naturally or normally. Finally, being able to work in a group is not necessarily very important in a job: being able to work on one's own or under a particular superior may be much more important.

Use of the interview for assessment

Ulrich and Trumbo in 1965 said:

> Apparently the interview is used almost universally as one of the sources of information on which personnel decisions of hiring, placement and in all likelihood transfer and promotion, are made. Because of its universality one would expect the interview to be the subject of a great deal of research and development effort. Furthermore one would expect its wide use and acceptance to be predicated on abundant empirical evidence of its predictive efficiency. However ... neither of these expectations is fulfilled in the literature.

Reliability

Before considering validity as such it is always as well to look at the reliability of a measure. In the case of the interview we are concerned with two kinds of reliability:

a Intra-individual reliability – does the same interviewer make the same assessment of the same candidate on two different occasions?

81

b Inter-individual reliability – do different interviewers make the same assessment of the same candidate?

In some studies of intra-individual reliability the interviewer has simply listened to a tape-recording of the interview at a later date and then made the same judgement. Sometimes he has interviewed the same candidate again at a later date. In either case reliabilities are relatively high, usually around 0·8 or 0·9 (e.g. Anderson 1954; Shaw 1952). The precise information obtained is likely to vary a little in these repeat interviews but the interviewers do use the same methods each time and investigate the same areas and apply the same weights to different kinds of information.

When we look at studies of inter-individual reliability then the correlations cited are noticeably lower. The original study. which demonstrated extreme inter-individual unreliability, was carried out by Scott in 1915. In this study six personnel managers each interviewed thirty-six salesmen and ranked them in order of suitability.

This was a more demanding task than is commonly presented to interviewers, who are usually only asked to rate each candidate on a scale with five to nine points on it. Under these conditions reliability is better: it is always better than chance and varies in different studies from ·15 to ·80 (Ulrich and Trumbo 1965). It is interesting in this context to compare inter-individual reliabilities for Board interviewing. These seem higher than for successive one-to-one interviews as one might expect: Zaccaria *et al.* (1956) estimated the reliability of their three-man boards at ·72 and correlations of between ·73 and ·97 have been found for Civil Service Promotion Board members (Hardinge 1974).

Mayfield (1964) has suggested that low inter-individual reliabilities may be due to four factors: 1. different interviewers cover different areas; 2. different weightings are given by different interviewers to the same information; 3. the information obtained is sometimes inaccurate; and 4. related to this, different kinds of behaviour by an interviewer will elicit different answers to questions by the interviewee. Mayfield quotes studies whose results support each of these conclusions. The higher reliabilities for Board interviewers follow clearly from this analysis, in that the only source of error open to them is to weight the answers to questions differently.

Validity

Any unreliability of the interview as a measure will reduce its apparent validity. And since the criteria used for assessing the predictive success of the interview are also likely to be unreliable measures, the interview itself is unlikely to emerge as a demonstrably valid procedure – and in general it does not.

Many of the studies of selection interviews do not differentiate clearly enough between judgements which the interviewer makes on the basis of the interview alone and judgements which are based on interview plus biographical information. In a normal selection procedure an interviewer will always have biographical information to look at before he carries out the selection interview. In an adequately designed study he will have to make an initial assessment based on the biographical information (together with test results or the results of group discussion techniques if used) and a subsequent assessment based on biographical information etc. plus interview information. Then each assessment can be compared with the criterion measurement of performance on the job or success in training. Few studies in fact meet these design criteria.

Kelly and Fiske (1951) examined the recruitment of graduate students to a training programme in clinical psychology. More than 500 graduates were involved and they were given a series of objective and projective tests followed by an interview of one or two hours. Information about their grades etc. was also available. When the biographical information was used alone for assessment, correlations of 0·24 were obtained with the students' success on the subsequent training programme. An interview raised the validity to 0·25. If test scores and biographical information were used together validity rose to 0·30. The interview could only raise this to 0·31. And this is a typical sort of finding.

Anderson (1954) reports more favourably on the validity of a carefully structured interview for prospective doctoral students. Here a thirty-minute interview raised validity from about ·20 (based on grades and recommendations of academic staff) to about ·50. This might possibly be due to the assessment of motivation in the interview and thus be linked to a review by Rimland (1960) of naval recruitment procedures, in which he concludes that career motivation is the one area where an interview aids prediction.

In some studies interviewers have been asked to rate candidates on particular traits rather than on overall suitability. They are more successful with some traits than with others. For example, in Bonneau's (1957) study interviewers tried to predict how well student teachers would establish rapport with schoolchildren. Their ratings were compared with actual ratings made by pupils and a correlation of ·65 was obtained. This was significantly higher than the correlations obtained by school principals who tried to predict the pupil ratings on the basis of their knowledge of the student teachers' work. Bonneau's interviews were highly structured with exactly the same questions being asked of all the student teachers and differential weightings being applied to the answers. Similarly Otis, Campbell and Prien (1962) concluded that of all the traits on which interviewers rated prospective employees they were only successful in predicting success in personal relationships.

Conclusions

What, then, is the value of including interviews in assessment procedures? Clearly they are not a particularly reliable source of information and their validity has not been demonstrated. Equally good results can usually be obtained by combining biographical data and test results. Only the personal relationships area seems to be better assessed by an interview, with a possibility that career motivation can also be usefully assessed.

Thus the value of the interview seems to be limited. It is, however, essential in certain situations: namely where a prospective employee is to work under one particular boss or where he is to join a closely interdependent team. It is essential in these circumstances that the new employee should get on well with the boss or that the other members of the team should have respect and liking for him. And these feelings are hard to predict from biographical information but easier to predict on the basis of an interview. This is close to the dimension of personal relationships that we have already discussed.

Interviews are also sometimes looked upon as a way of 'selling' an organization. No one wants to work for a firm where he does not know anyone and which he feels is not sufficiently interested in staff to want to see them before taking them on. Again the interview is being used in a personal relationship context.

Of recent years we have learned more of what goes on in an interview and this has enabled us to find out a certain amount about the relationships between interviewer and interviewee behaviour. As a result of this interviewing training has improved a good deal and it may be that, as a result of improved techniques, interviewers are now rather better at using the interview to find out what they need to know. The next section presents a brief résumé of advances in this area and the reader may judge for himself whether or not such knowledge is likely to increase the reliability and validity of interviews.

Interviewing training

As little as ten years ago the theoretical content of a course on interviewing typically consisted of a list of some ten or twenty tips on interviewing. These tips would begin with the importance of making a plan for the interview beforehand, of 'putting the candidate at ease', and 'establishing rapport', would proceed through some examples of how to phrase questions and finish with a recommendation to let the candidate ask any questions he wishes. These tips would be based on generalized personal experience of what makes an interview go well.

The situation today is a rather different one. Knowledge is slowly accumulating on the relationships between interviewer behaviour and the subsequent responses of the interviewee. There are certain objectives which research evidence can help the interviewer achieve.

OBJECTIVE	RECOMMENDATION WHICH CAN BE MADE ON THE BASIS OF RESEARCH EVIDENCE
1. Get interviewee to talk more	i. Place chairs at a comfortable distance apart and almost directly face to face (Mehrabian and Diamond, 1971).
	There is some current controversy on this point. Argyle (1972, p. 39) concluded on the basis of some rather indirect evidence that relaxed conversation is encouraged by seating angle of 90°–120°.
	ii. Look interviewee in the eye and smile as you ask a question or as you reach the end of what you have to say (Argyle 1972, pp. 82–6).

	iii. Do not interrupt (Chapple, 1956) or leave long pauses (Gorden, 1956). iv. Ask open-ended questions (Dohrenwend and Richardson, 1965). v. Adopt active attitude; talking about self, giving own views etc. (Heller *et al.*, 1966; Jourard, 1971).
2. Get interviewee to <u>enlarge</u> on <u>topic</u>	i. Make encouraging noises (Krasner, 1958; Salzinger and Pisoni, 1960). ii. Disagree with him (Davis 1971). There is an apparent conflict here which disappears when it is recognized that Davis does not in fact disagree very often, and that making an encouraging noise is not the same thing as agreeing with what has been said.
3. <u>Get interviewee</u> to <u>stop talking or to change</u> topic	i. Agree with him (Davis, 1971). ii. Look away from him (Argyle, 1972). iii. Sit forward, move arms forward (Kendon, 1972).
4. Get accurate in- <u>formation</u>	i. Ask open-ended questions (Moscovici, 1963). ii. Ask probing questions (Guest, 1947). The evidence appears to conflict here but some of the conflict disappears if it is appreciated that the normal thing to do is to ask an open-ended question first in order to obtain a spontaneous response and follow this up with probing closed questions in order to obtain precise information on a particular matter. iii. Ask leading questions of an adult (Richardson, 1960) but non-leading questions of a child (Stern, 1938).

Evidence on this subject is again superficially in conflict but again the conflict is more apparent than real once it is recognized that leading questions, while obtaining misleading information from the suggestible, can clarify issues for the more intelligent.

iv. Avoid the more obvious sources of interviewer bias by selecting unbiased, unexceptional interviewers and then training them (Kahn and Cannell, 1957).

NB. Main sources and reviews have been given as references whenever possible, and individual studies which merely confirm a theory have been deliberately omitted.

With this kind of information the interviewer is in a better position to control the responses of the interviewee. He is likely to be able to get the interviewee talking on relevant subjects and he may get more accurate and precise information from him. This goes part of the way towards improving the reliability and validity of an interview. It will be remembered that Mayfield (1964) concluded that low inter-individual reliabilities are partly due to inaccurate information being obtained and that different information was obtained depending upon interviewer behaviour. Improved training of interviewers based on the kind of evidence cited above should improve the situation.

In other areas of the interview we are less able to use research evidence to improve the quality of interviewing. The use which is made of information obtained is crucial, for example, but we are far from knowing how to weight information obtained in order to reach the 'best' decision. This problem is discussed in chapter 9.

8
Vocational counselling

Vocational counselling is the process of helping people to make occupational decisions: helping people to choose the occupation, the profession, the training or educational course that will suit them best. Rodger and Cavanagh (1962, have described the process as follows:

> There is much to be said for envisaging the basic vocational guidance task as a double one with both positive and negative aims. The negative aim is gently to steer people away from wòrk likely to prove unsuitable to their capacities or inclinations or both. The positive aim is to supply information about apparently suitable occupations and to foster an attitude of 'planned procrastination' in the consideration of them.

In order to do this most theorists consider it is necessary first to be able to assess the individual. Super and Crites (1962) have said:

> Vocational counselling has two fundamental purposes: to help people make good vocational adjustments and to

facilitate smooth functioning of the economy through the effective use of manpower. These purposes imply that each individual has certain abilities, interests, personality traits and other characteristics which, if he knows them and their potential value, will make him a happier man, a more effective worker and a more useful citizen.

So for vocational counselling it is necessary to have the fullest possible picture of a particular individual. There is no one aptitude or personality characteristic that we are looking for and we are as much concerned with the relative strengths of an individual's aptitudes as we are with his strengths in relation to a particular comparison group. So we tend to look for rather different tools of assessment.

Assessing aptitudes

Here we look for batteries of tests which offer us measures of the relative strengths of different aptitudes rather than individual unrelated tests of each one – even though the separate tests may be better standardized. So in assessing abilities we are likely to choose either the DAT (for school-leavers or students trying to decide on a course of further education) or the GATB (for school-leavers or adults who are more concerned about choosing a job than a course). These batteries of tests give us an overall picture of an individual's aptitudes and enable us to perceive his *relative* strengths and weaknesses.

Sometimes this may not be what is required: a particular individual may have come for counselling having already decided upon a preferred occupation. He may wish to be an engineer and simply be concerned to discover whether he has sufficient aptitude for it. In this case it would not be helpful to give tests of language ability or of clerical speed and accuracy. It would be more helpful to choose a test of mechanical reasoning which has been standardized on an appropriate comparison group. This will give him a better idea of how successful he is likely to be.

There are limitations on the usefulness of assessing abilities in vocational counselling. One limitation is that many of the important job aptitudes are not measured by standardized tests. We do not know how to assess an individual's aptitude for teaching, or for arranging flowers, or for being a vet. We can test for some of the aptitudes involved in these jobs but not for the total job. In very few cases is there a simple and direct relationship between the aptitude measured and the job to be carried out. Often the best predictor will be a test of intelligence, or general learning ability in new situations.

Ability also interacts with motivation in determining job satisfaction and job success, and it can be argued that over a lengthy period of time the motivation is more important than the aptitude. If we examine the correlations in Table 8.1 we see that although tests of clerical ability were good predictors of training success for clerks they were not as good at predicting performance on the job as were tests of personality.

Table 8.1 Validity coefficients for general clerks (adapted from Ghiselli 1973)

Tests	Training	Performance
Intellectual	0·47	0·28
Perceptual Accuracy	0·36	0·27
Personality/ interests	0·17	0·30

In vocational counselling assessing motivation tends to be equated with assessing areas of interest: an assumption seems to be made that if an individual is doing a job which interests him he will work hard and achieve satisfaction. Tests of 'general motivation' or ambition, like tests of persistence or need for achievement, are not normally employed, therefore; more surprisingly, nor are tests of differential motivation like the MAT or the TAT. It would seem that a profile of needs, showing the relative importance for an individual of, say, achievement, affiliation, money and power, could be a useful tool in counselling.

However the MAT does not in fact throw much light on work motivation and the TAT takes a long time and needs an expert interpreter, so perhaps it is not so surprising that interest tests are used. And some tests of interests do come close to measuring motivation in a general sense.

The Allport–Vernon Study of Values is one of these and this was described in Chapter 4. Super (1962, 1973) has developed a Work Values Inventory which examines values more appropriate to work situations. Factors emerge from this which are familiar to us from our knowledge of motivation at work. One of these is the 'security-economic returns-surroundings-supervisory relations' value which reminds us very much of Herzberg's hygiene factor in work motivation. A second is doubtfully labelled 'goodness of life' and includes such aspects as 'altruism-associates-aesthetics-surroundings and achievement'. A third is recognizably Herzberg's motivator factor with 'creativity-variety-intellectual stimulation'. The fourth is concerned with 'independence-management-prestige'. This inventory is still in an experimental stage and is described here because the area is not covered by any established measuring instrument.

All tests of interests are concerned to some extent, however, with the intrinsic rewards to be found in different areas of work. The most widely used and influential is probably the Kuder Vocational Preference Record. From three suggested activities the individual chooses the one he would most enjoy and the one he would least enjoy, e.g.

compile a dictionary of slang
discover a cure for hay fever
install improved office procedures
 in a big business

The responses to 168 questions of this type yield a profile of preferences for activities in different interest areas. Thus a particular individual might obtain a profile like that in Fig 8.1. The Kuder is an American test and so are the norms supplied. Although we have argued that this is less important in vocational counselling than in selection there is no doubt that any peculiarities in the standardization sample can lead to exaggeratedly high or low scores in particular areas. The Kuder has an additional peculiarity which is that high scores on literary interest in particular, *but also* on musical and artistic, may sometimes indicate neuroticism rather than genuine interest.

There are English tests of interests also, standardized on English samples. One which has been widely used by careers officers and careers teachers in this country is the Rothwell–Miller (1968). This is constructed quite differently to the Kuder. The individual ranks twelve occupations in preferred order and does this, with different occupations, nine times.

Here is a typical list:

Dance band leader	Radio mechanic
Youth employment officer	Accounts clerk
Postal clerk	Geologist
Plumber	Publicity officer
Physiotherapist	Window dresser
Transport driver	Radio scriptwriter

Again responses yield a 'profile' of interest areas – only this time the areas are simply ranked in order of preference and include a medical interest area. As a test the Rothwell-

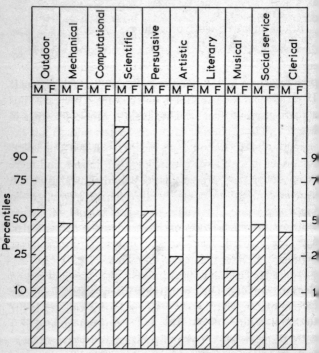

Fig. 8.1 *The Kuder Vocational Preference Record (adapted from Kuder, 1951)*

Miller has two important disadvantages. One is that it is really quite difficult to rate twelve occupations in order of preference and it is doubtful whether more than the top and bottom two ratings have much meaning. Another difficulty is that there are separate forms for males (blue) and females (pink). This is hardly consonant with current social attitudes on sex discrimination, quite apart from the fact that a number of occupations are thus unnecessarily and pointlessly omitted from each form. The best use of the Rothwell–Miller is probably as a basis for discussion of the client's attitude towards specific occupations rather than as a way of clearly determining areas of interest. It can certainly suggest some interesting areas of discussion with rather silent school-leavers. And it does have some predictive validity. Young people (particularly boys) who entered an occupation which was consonant with their preferences on the Rothwell–Miller were found (Nelson 1968) to remain in it longer and to hold a more positive attitude towards it. Differences were significant but not large.

More recently (1969), the Applied Psychology Unit at the University of Edinburgh have developed a test of vocational interests which follows the Kuder pretty closely in design. Advantages of the APU Occupational Interests Guide are that (1) it is considerably shorter than the Kuder, and (2) there are different versions available to suit different ages and levels of intelligence (some of the Kuder questions and Rothwell–Miller occupations are somewhat obscure). Disadvantages are: (1) like the Rothwell–Miller there are different forms for males and females, and (2) factor-analysis reveals a combined clerical/sales area rather than two separate areas. This is due to the inclusion of a number of jobs which involve both clerical and sales components (like calculating the weekly takings in a shop). It is therefore likely to create confusion in counsellors since the personality characteristics necessary for sales are very different from those for clerical workers. Nor are the same aptitudes involved.

In America there is another classic interest inventory – The Strong Vocational Interest Blank, now revised as the Strong–Campbell Interest Inventory. This yields two kinds of information. In addition to scores in six general occupational themes and 23 basic interest areas, scores are also compared directly with the typical patterns of interests shown by people in different occupations, see Fig. 8.2. There are currently about sixty of these occupational profiles available. Simply, the counsellor compares an individual's profile with that of typical people in particular occupations and selects the ones which 'fit' best. This process demands the use of a computer and even when accomplished is not entirely satisfactory since the available profiles do not adequately cover the field of employment opportunities. It also assumes that all parts of the profile are equally important for success and adjustment in the particular occupation, though this is unlikely to be the case.

In practice the SVIB seems to have much the same kind of validity as the Rothwell–Miller. Here is what David Campbell says of the male version:

Certain information derived from administering the inventory does point to its general validity. For instance, college students were identified who scored very high on the sales occupational scales as high-school seniors; 10 years later 10% of them were selling life insurance and 32% were selling something else. Therefore 40% of them did become salesmen. Another 12% of them were in business – persuasion types of jobs – public relations, marketing – and 22% were in social service – persuasive jobs such as minister, school teacher or lawyer. These are all people-oriented occupations. 24% were in occupations

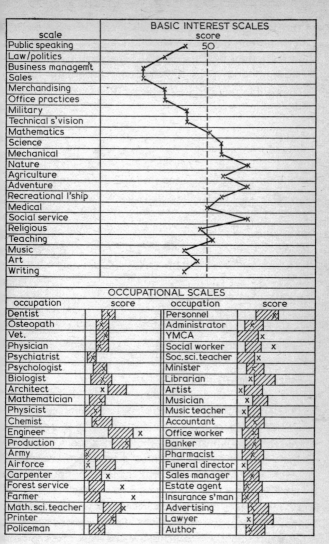

Fig. 8.2 *Adapted from Profile Sheet for the Strong Vocational Interest Blank for Men (1969) – some occupations omitted*

that appeared unrelated to their profile 10 years earlier. The hit-rate here was about 3 to 1. This ratio appears often in the SVIB literature and suggests that in general about 75% of college students wind up in jobs that are compatible with their earlier SVIB profile. (1973: 48–9)

In evaluating this kind of evidence two points must be borne in mind. Firstly, the college students will have been told of their scores. They have thus been 'advised' as to the job or type of occupation they will do best in or be best satisfied with. This makes it more likely that they will enter just such an occupation. Secondly, we should not expect interests to remain completely stable over long periods of time. Some of these young people should have changed their area of interest quite a bit over a ten-year period, and we should expect them to be in quite different occupations to those predicted. It is therefore virtually impossible to evaluate validation studies on interest tests since we do not know how predictive we really want them to be.

Assessment and counselling

Changes in self-estimate

How helpful is individual assessment in the vocational counselling process? Do clients, for example, change their self-estimates after learning the results of tests they have taken? Goldman (1961) reviewed a series of studies in this area and concluded: 1. estimates of vocational interests are more susceptible to change than are estimates of ability or personality; 2. group procedures for feeding back test results lead to greater changes in self-estimates; 3. most changes were short-lived. Later studies have been consistent with these conclusions and have mainly been concerned with comparing different ways of giving test information. Holmes (1964), for example, found that mailed information was remembered well but not highly valued; Tipton (1969) that a Skinnerian learning programme produced better initial learning than a counsellor but that a month later the counselled group showed greater change.

The assumption seems to be made in almost all the studies carried out that any change in self-estimate in the direction of the results shows an increased accuracy of self-assessment. This probably accounts for the apparent 'superiority' of non-counsellor mediated communication of results. Few counsellors would encourage their clients to believe all the test results tell them. Those that do are surely not good counsellors and do not in fact help their clients improve the accuracy of their self-estimates. Errors occur for many reasons: instructions not being fully understood, imperfections in the design of the instruments themselves, scoring errors and genuine inconsistencies in the behaviour of the client. Interpretation by the counsellor of test results will therefore usually lead clients to place less reliance on them.

Appropriateness of vocational choice

Most studies of the relationship between test results and vocational choice are undertaken by the authors of the tests themselves. They 'validate' the test in terms of the number of subjects who choose occupations congruent with the test results (*c.f.* Campbell's study of the SVIB which has already been discussed). There is no attempt made to ascertain whether vocational choices have *changed* as a result of hearing the test results.

However, those studies which have attempted to measure vocational preferences before and after the communication of test results do find changes occurring and in the direction of congruence (e.g. Hoyt 1955, Pilato 1968, Williams and Hills 1962). Pilato, who administered both a test of intelligence and of interests, found that the changes which occurred were mainly in level of occupation rather than in the area chosen; he hypothesized that the intelligence test scores were simply easier to remember.

Later stages in counselling

Interpretation of test scores

It is important to stress that assessment of the individual is only the beginning of vocational counselling. We have already touched on the problems of interpreting the results of psychological tests. On the one hand we do want clients to take notice of them and to incorporate them into their estimates or concepts of themselves; on the other hand we want them to be aware of possible inaccuracies. Suppose mistakes have been made in scoring? Suppose we actually have someone else's scores in front of us? This may happen in only one of a thousand cases, but in counselling each individual is of ultimate and absolute importance. The counsellor must be sufficiently open in his own attitudes to be able to recognize when scores are wrong.

Apart from these rare cases, how can clients be helped in evaluating and using test scores?

Aptitudes. In the case of tests of aptitude, scores are usually given in terms of percentiles: whether the individual falls within the top 1, 5, 25 per cent etc. of a given population. The concept of a percentile, or even of a percentage, is often not understood. The counsellor must be able to explain. Then the characteristics of the sample population must be explained. How directly relevant is it to the population with which the client needs to be able to compare himself? The additional problem of male and female scores may enter in here. Clearly the client is usually in competition with a mixed-sex group. Comparing herself with the very low female norms on spatial or mechanical reasoning might mislead a prospective female engineer badly.

The counsellor must also be able to explain the different significance of high and low scores. While a high score may be taken at its face value a low score may not. The low score may be the result of a temporary loss of concentration or the misunderstanding of instructions: the high score could not have been achieved by chance alone. The interaction between ability and motivation must also be made clear to the client.

Interests and values. Tests of interests and values are easier to interpret. For one thing the client has a much better idea of his or her own interests and is therefore less likely to be misled by odd results. And the tests themselves usually offer a self-interpretative leaflet which helps. The main difficulty in interpretation is to know and to convey the degree to which apparent high and low points in a profile are significant, or the extent to which similarity to a given occupational profile implies success and satisfaction in that particular role. Zytowski (1973) says 'such statements as "You ought to be a ..." or "You will regret it if you don't ..." are too strong for what interest inventories yield'. There is no way round this. Although manuals offer sophisticated data in terms of the significance of certain scores, significance really remains in the eye of the client. A score which confirms a previous expectation has, quite rightly, a significance which exceeds that of a statistically 'significant' but incomprehensible score.

Counselling and psychotherapy
Some theorists (e.g. Patterson 1969) do not perceive vocational counselling as being essentially different from other

forms of psychotherapy and therefore consider that the same principles apply. These principles usually imply that the counsellor will be a great deal less directive than we have so far assumed. For example, Carl Rogers has said:

> We do not diagnose his (the client's) case, nor evaluate his personality; we do not prescribe treatment nor determine what changes are to be effected, nor set the goal that shall be defined as the cure. Instead the therapist approaches the client with a genuine respect for the person he now is and with a continuing appreciation of him as he changes during the association. He tries to see the client as the client sees himself, to look at problems through his eyes, to perceive with him his confusions, fears and ambitions. The therapist in such a relationship is not concerned with judging or making suggestions, but always strives to understand. In this atmosphere of complete psychological security, the client can lay himself bare with no danger of being hurt. Protected by the conditions of therapy, he begins to re-organise the structure of self in accordance with reality and his own needs. (*Scientific American*, 1952)

Although this was written of psychotherapy in general, it comes very close to the aims of the vocational counsellor. Super (1953) has stated these as follows: 'Development through life stages can be guided partly by facilitating the maturation of abilities and interests and partly by aiding in reality testing and the development of the self-concept.' The difference lies only in the extent to which the counsellor is perceived as directive.

Those who have seen vocational counselling more in terms of help in decision-making would also see the counsellor as being non-directive (Rodger and Kavanagh 1962; Krumboltz and Thoresen 1969). Krumboltz and Thoresen, (p. 293) describe programmed learning packages to help high-school children understand what is involved in doing different kinds of jobs, and Varenhorst (Krumboltz and Thoresen, p. 306) describes a Life Career Game in which children learn the consequences of taking certain decisions at certain stages in life.

Undoubtedly the counselling situation *is* different from the psychotherapeutic situation. Stefflre (1965) describes some of the differences as follows:

Goals:
The goals of counselling are more limited and more focused upon immediate changes in behaviour. They are also more concerned with adopting social roles and with the development of abilities.

Clients:
The clients of the counsellor are more likely to be psychologically well-adjusted.

Practitioners:
Counsellors are likely to have received less training.

Settings:
Counselling more often occurs in the educational setting of school or college.

Methods and Instruments:
Counselling is concerned with the present and future rather than with effects of the past. A cognitive change rather than an affective one is sought; and a reduction in ambiguity rather than an increase.

9
Personnel selection

The application of psychological tests and measures in the selection of people for jobs has a long history in the development of applied psychology. That is to say it goes back some sixty years. Intelligence tests were first used on a large scale in the selection of personnel for the US Army in the First World War. Millions of men were screened and allocated to training and jobs where they could become operationally effective as soon as possible. A few industrial organizations employed selection tests during the 1920s and 1930s, but use before the Second World War was still quite rare. Psychological selection techniques were used extensively by the services in the 1939–45 war, both in the USA and in the UK, and since then their application has spread widely in industry.

As shown in Chapter 1, selection is best viewed as one stage in the process of induction and preparation for work. The first step in setting up a procedure for selection is to analyse and describe the job (or more frequently the category of jobs) for which personnel are required.

Job descriptions vary between the simplest statements (e.g. 'young lad wanted to deliver groceries') to lengthy descriptions based upon detailed analysis of the decision procedures and skills required for successful completion of the tasks. The latter can only be obtained by analysing the job. There are a range of techniques now available for doing this. They normally take the form of systematic interviews with, or questionnaire completion by, the current job holders and/or their supervisors. Observational methods are often used to supplement the information obtained. The critical incident technique, originally proposed by J. C. Flanagan (1949), has been frequently used. The technique elicits descriptions of actual incidences where outstanding good or particularly unsatisfactory performance occurred. A large number of incidents are required from a cross section of the work force in order to establish a stable basis for deciding what traits may be involved. Some forms of job analysis take into consideration the relative importance of different tasks (e.g. what is the cost of failure?), their difficulty and their frequency of occurrence.

Job analysis techniques have in the main been developed to meet the needs of trainers rather than selectors. The techniques elicit performance requirements of the job. This is what is required for the selection of people already trained for the job. For example, if you want a shorthand typist and you are seeking a trained person a performance test in these skills will determine suitability. If, on the other hand, one wishes to assess whether a girl with no training has the potential to be a good shorthand typist some other form of assessment is required. Thus while job analysis can establish the *performance* requirements of the job, there is still the task of translating these into the *aptitudes* required to attain the appropriate level of performance. There is no systematic procedure for doing this at present. The best one can do is to choose psychological tests which seem to tap the same fundamental intellectual or performance operations as the job itself.

Another area in which job analysis is currently weak is in determining the personality and interest requirements of the job although the critical incident technique often indicates the social and motivational causes of success and failure in the job. A somewhat different approach is to examine characteristics of the employees currently employed on the job and particularly the characteristics of those rated as successful and how they differ from the less successful. When supervisors are asked what discriminates between their best and worst workers, motivation and reliability often figure more prominently than differences in skill.

Advertising

Having obtained, by one means or another, the requirements of the job, recruiting can begin. The next step is to advertise either from within the organization or from outside for candidates. The way in which the advertisement is framed is important in getting the right people to apply. The advertisement should obviously be as accurate as possible but the standards required should not sound so high that able candidates are discouraged or so low that hundreds of applications may be received for each vacancy – which would waste the time of applicants and selectors alike.

Screening

Screening simply means cutting down the number of applicants to a manageable size before the next stage in a selection procedure. If the number of applicants is small it may be unnecessary to do other than eliminate the obviously unsuitable by virtue of age and experience. If the numbers are large, other criteria must be applied in screening. Some more elaborate forms of selection occupy two stages, and psychological tests may be used in the screening process in addition to the final selection procedure. It is clearly important to the organization carrying out the selection procedure that candidates who are likely to succeed are not rejected because insufficient information is available to make a rational decision. It is also important for the individual candidates that selection is based upon a fair and rational basis.

Selection

Assuming the field of applicants has now been reduced to a manageable number, a full assessment of the remaining candidates can be made. The cost of the procedure cannot of course be ignored. The cost of each additional bit of information collected should be weighed against the likely benefits in terms of increased accuracy in selection decisions. This at least is the theory. In practice one can usually only make a very rough guess as to the likely benefits from adding another test or an extra interview to the procedure.

In building up a selection procedure measures should be chosen to assess all the characteristics of the candidates which were considered necessary during the process of job analysis. Let us assume we are selecting policemen. We might find from an analysis of the job that a relatively high intelligence was required and a mildly authoritarian and extrovert personality considered to make an effective policeman. The assessment of these dimensions could all be made with paper-and-pencil psychological tests. The job description might also call for a certain pattern of interests and this could be assessed by a test of interests (see Ch. 8).

The appearance and social skills of a policeman are important and these could be best assessed in an interview. Finally an indication of the candidate's integrity would be called for and this might be best obtained from his previous record and character references.

Although the battery of measures initially chosen for selection is based upon an analysis of the job, the battery should be given a trial run to test its validity before it is used for selection. One way in which this could be achieved is by administering the battery to a sample of, say, 200 police constables who have served in the force for at least two years. Their scores on the various tests and interviews could then be related to an assessment of their performance as policemen. The problem with such a 'concurrent' validity study is that it does not necessarily provide a good indication of the *predictive* validity, which is what we are really interested in. The performance on the battery of tests of policemen who have been in the force for some time is likely to be different from that which they would have scored when joining. The interests of the policeman are likely to have changed, and there may be some shift in his score on the authoritarian scale. He would almost certainly appear more mature and confident in an interview.

A more suitable form of validation study is one in which the battery of measures is tried out on a sample of new entrants to the police force and the scores are correlated with performance after one year of service. This of course means waiting at least a year before any results are available. Table 9.1 provides an example of the correlations which may be obtained from such a study. (These figures are based upon an actual validation study of policemen carried out by Helen Jessup although the circumstances were different and not all the measures shown were employed.)

	Performance Rating
	Correlation
Intelligence	0·34
Authoritarian Personality	0·42
Extraversion	0·37
Neuroticism	−0·41
Interests Scale	0·28
Appearance	0·14
Social Skills	0·18

The results show that all the measures tested are significantly correlated with success as a policeman although the correlations for the two ratings obtained from the interview (appearance, social skills) are quite low. Neuroticism is negatively correlated, as expected, which means that it is the less neurotic (i.e. more stable) policemen who are successful.

The next problem we face is how we could use this information to make selection decisions. While all the measures are potentially of some value, some are better predictors of success than others. Fortunately there is a statistical technique available for combining scores to give an overall best prediction – this is multiple regression. The procedure is relatively complex and will not be worked through here (see G. H. Thomson 1951 for a description of the method). Multiple regression produces 'weightings' to apply to the test scores to give the best-combined predictor of success. The correlation between this value and success is known as the 'multiple correlation' (R). Let us assume the multiple correlation in the above study is $R = 0.59$. (R cannot be calculated directly from the data in Table 9.1 as the intercorrelations between all the measures are required.)

Although a correlation provides a useful index to summarize the relationship between two variables, what is required for practical purposes is to be able to predict the chances of success of candidates from their performance in the selection situation. This provides an estimate of the utility of the proposed selection system.

Correlations can be transposed into expectancy charts by the use of a set of tables (Taylor–Russell tables, see Taylor and Russell 1939). A table can also be compiled directly from the data collected in the validation study by analysing the success rate on the job in relation to score levels obtained from the selection battery. In the case of our policemen the expectancy chart would look like that shown in Table 9.2. For the sake of simplicity we have classified performance as a policeman as simply successful and unsuccessful. Success would be defined as scoring above a certain point on the performance scale for policemen.

An expectancy chart such as this would clearly be extremely valuable to a selection panel. Not only could decisions be made on individual candidates based upon an estimate of his probability of success but the overall success rate of any entry to the police force could be easily calculated. If a specified number of recruits were required for the police force, as many as possible would be selected from the higher score categories to maximize the number of successful ones. If recruiting were difficult and few candidates were available to choose from, it might be necessary to drop entry standards and take men in, say, the 20–24 category with only slightly more than a 50–50 chance of being successful. This is an administrative decision.

A point to note in the expectancy chart is that the success or failure of any individual cannot be predicted with certainty from the information available to selectors. Even those who score very high and seemingly have all the attributes occasionally fail. At the other end of the scale,

Table 9.2 Expectancy chart – policemen

Combined score on Selection Battery converted to 50 point scale	Percent successful
42–50	95%
35–41	80%
30–34	70%
25–29	62%
20–24	52%
below 20	not sufficient data available

for which we do not have data available in this example, experience shows that even from the lowest categories of scores some successes are recorded. This is partly because there is some degree of error in our measuring instruments and particular individuals may be misclassified. More important is the fact that selection batteries can never adequately cover all the important requirements of a job. The battery described in the above example does not measure motivation adequately although the measure of interests and the interview would touch upon some aspects of it. Motivation is difficult to measure and it is not necessarily stable over time. But no one will doubt that individuals very keen and very determined to succeed in a situation can partially compensate for a lack of the other qualities normally associated with success in that situation. Conversely, the man who scores very high on our battery of tests but who is poorly motivated may well fail.

Returning to the validation study in which we tested policemen entering the force and compared their results with performance a year or so later, one weakness of such an exercise is that no information is available on the candidates who were not accepted. The validation study was limited to those initially considered acceptable. We do not know what the success rate of the rejected candidates would have been. The ideal validation study from a research viewpoint would be one in which all applicants for a job were tested on the experimental battery but the scores were ignored and all were selected for the job. If the numbers were too large the selection of candidates should be made at random. We would then be able to assess the later performance of candidates at all levels of potential. Probability estimates of success could be calculated for all categories of candidates. For obvious practical reasons, few studies of this type have ever been carried out.

It should be noted that in the above example in which the scores on a number of different tests and ratings were added (after appropriate weighting) to get the overall prediction of success, the implicit assumption was made that a high score on one of the measures compensates for a low score on another. In practice this seems a reasonable assumption to make, although it is a gross oversimplification. But a number of selection systems do stipulate minimum criteria on certain tests if these characteristics are considered critical for success. For example, a highly intelligent person may score high on all the tests and measures in a selection procedure for engineers except on mechanical aptitude in which he scores very low. In this circumstance one might be doubtful as to his success as an engineer. The chances of his staying in the profession would also be rated as low. He would be better advised to try some other career. (Assessment on a selection battery can provide useful vocational guidance information if fed back to the candidate.) In the policemen example, one might question the selection of candidates who score very high on the neuroticism scale even if they were rated highly in other respects.

Again, if the character references taken up on candidates for the police force, which have not been included as part of the battery, were negative and there was supporting data to doubt the candidate's integrity, these would normally imply rejection of the candidate even if he scored highly on other parts of the selection system.

The interview also is often used to veto the selection of a candidate irrespective of his scores on other parts of the selection procedure. From many studies which demonstrate the low validity of interview assessments this is a doubtful practice. Nevertheless, it is difficult to convince managers to select candidates that they personally judge to be unsuitable.

Medical examinations which often express suitability for employment in Yes-No terms where used are often seen as something distinct from the rest of the selection procedure. In fact, predictions of future states of health (and employability) from a medical examination are not necessarily more valid than the predictions of performance from psychological tests. There are instances where it may be worth considering incorporating medical predictions in the overall equation to determine the selection decision.

A second example of a validation exercise conducted by the authors is quoted to illustrate some further features of psychological selection – Jessup and Jessup (1971). The Eysenck Personality Inventory (EPI) was given experimentally to 205 pilot cadets on entry to the RAF: The sample had already survived a highly elaborate system of selection lasting some three days. The EPI was tried out to see if the addition of this new measure could improve prediction.

As shown in Chapter 3 populations can be divided into four quadrants according to whether they are above or below average on neuroticism and extraversion respectively. The percentage of the pilot cadets who succeeded in passing through initial flying training and advanced flying training without being failed or recoursed is shown in Fig. 9.1.

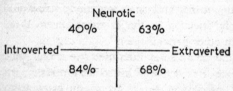

Fig. 9.1 *First time success rate of pilot cadets*

It can be seen that the success rate is highest among the stable introverts and lowest among the neurotic introverts. The differences are quite striking when it is considered that these personality dimensions can only explain part of the reason for success or failure; many intellectual and psychomotor factors are known to be important.

A further check was made to see whether or not the measures of extraversion and neuroticism were measuring something new or just repeating something that was already being measured by part of the existing selection battery. It was found that the correlations between the extraversion and neuroticism scores and the pilot index (the combined selection index) were small and not statistically significant.

Further, when a subsample of pilots who were successful was matched in terms of pilot index scores against a subsample who had failed, the similar significant relationship was still found. That is to say, the success rate was highest for the stable introverts and lowest among the neurotic introverts. This finding indicates that the EPI could make the prediction of success in flying training more accurate if the same results could be repeated.

A possible explanation for this result is that stable introverts are more readily 'conditioned' and thus learn more quickly than neurotic extroverts. A second hypothesis is required to explain the high failure rate among neurotic introverts, but this could be more easily explained in terms of the high anxiety experienced by this group, particularly in response to a potentially stressful situation such as flying training. For a discussion on these points see Jessup and Jessup (1971).

What the above study does illustrate is that understanding how different types of personality relate to success at work is far from simple. If we are to make more use of measures of personality in selection in the future we shall have to adopt more sophisticated models of behaviour to predict performance at work. While it seems reasonable to assume that high levels of intelligence and aptitudes are an advantage, or at least not a disadvantage, in tackling most of the problems met at work, there are no such simple assumptions that can be made with regard to personality dimensions. Being an extravert may be a definite asset in the performance of some tasks at work but a disadvantage in performing other tasks, even within the same job. There is also a real danger in validating personality measures against training criteria alone. One could imagine that to succeed in induction training to an organization a potential manager needs to conform, accept and learn procedures and so on. Yet when trained the company need a quite different personality – one who is going to innovate and be creative. Actually few companies do *want* such people but they certainly *need* them.

The use of psychological tests in selection decreases as the age and experience of the candidates increases. Psychological tests are primarily measures of potential and are of most value for selecting staff at the beginning or during the early stages of their careers. When they have worked for some years their achievement provides an additional source from which to predict future behaviour. Achievement should be assessed in relation to opportunities to provide maximum information on future potential. Unfortunately there has been very little attempt systematically to utilize the past performance of individuals to predict future behaviour. It is still very much a matter of making common sense judgements.

Psychological tests still have a part to play in selection even among people of middle age if they are changing careers or planning to make significant changes in their roles. The tests can measure attributes which they have had little chance of demonstrating.

It is not by accident that the two validation studies of selection quoted in this chapter refer to large organizations which take in many recruits to be trained for the same category of job. These are the circumstances which allow an effective selection system to be developed and also where the potential pay-off from the system is high. It is seldom practical in small organizations to validate selection procedures to develop estimates of likely success in the job. Nevertheless a selection procedure can be devised, starting with a job analysis, in which tests are chosen to measure the qualities considered important. While there is no scientific way of setting minimum criteria on such a battery it will still provide useful information on the relative strengths of a group of candidates. If the tests have been normalized on a national population it will also provide information on the relative strengths and weaknesses of an individual and how he relates to the national norm.

Alternative selection models

The traditional selection model is based on the assumption that people work in clearly prescribed jobs. This is perhaps a reasonable assumption to make with respect to the majority of jobs in British industry and is the reason why the psychological methods of selection which have been adopted have met with a fair degree of success. Many jobs on the other hand allow the incumbent a good deal of scope in the way in which he tackles the job and even, to some extent, in the objectives he pursues. Most senior jobs fall into this category but so do a minority of jobs at lower levels within organizations.

The distinction has been drawn by Burns and Stalker (1961) between mechanistic and organistic organizations. The mechanistic organization is one in which there is considerable division of labour into specialized tasks, a clear hierarchy of authority and precisely defined jobs with lots of rules and regulations related to the conduct of work. This description is close to Weber's (1947) conception of the ideal bureaucracy. Organistic organizations operate more flexibly. There could be a continual redefinition of individual jobs as the situation requires. Individual employees have greater discretion in the conduct of their work and decisions are in general taken on lower levels within the organization. The selection model we have described previously is more applicable to mechanistic organizations because the requirements of particular jobs can be specified more precisely.

If jobs can be tackled in a variety of ways, different skills and capacities may be brought into use by different job holders. Employees would tend to adopt a style of working to suit their own capacities and personality. This is very reasonable and desirable but it presents problems to selectors. It means that different combinations of attributes may lead to success. If this situation exists (and in fact it exists in all jobs to a greater or lesser extent) it would become apparent in the analysis of the job requirements. When the job holders are interviewed the relative importance they attach to different aspects of the job will vary.

The implications for selection are that a higher order of generality must be aimed at in assessing aptitudes and personality. If the job has a technical content it is probable that some minimal level of aptitude for the appropriate technical area will be required and higher levels of the aptitude will be a positive advantage. The personality requirements for such roles may be more complicated. For example, one man may succeed because he is an extravert while a second may succeed by adopting a style which suits his introverted personality. In this case extraversion could not be used to discriminate between success and failure in this job. The difficulties for selecting for certain types of personality has already been discussed.

The ultimate test of the selection model adopted is of course the validation study. That is why it is so important to check whether the selection procedure adopted actually works in relation to later performance at work.

10
Manpower planning

A recent development in the thinking in personnel departments of large organizations has been to integrate their procedures for recruitment of staff, selection, training, career development and promotion into an overall plan. The plan must take into account significant events and changes in the organization over the next five, ten or perhaps twenty years. To be able to plan effectively it is necessary to estimate the staff needs of the organization by level and skill category at various points in the future.

In the absence of such planning, as many know to their cost, organizations find that as they change and introduce new technological developments there is a serious mismatch between the skills their employees possess and those which are required to operate efficiently. They may find they have an abundance of workers in certain skill categories while having severe shortages in others. They may find that some of their key workers are on the point of retirement and that no one has been trained to replace them. Although retirements are largely predictable, other forms of personnel wastage through changing jobs is less so although in large established organizations it is possible to obtain estimates of the likely labour turnover among particular categories of employee.

For successful manpower planning it is necessary to be able to estimate the manpower needs of the organization at certain times in the future. Perhaps annual forecasts are made. The second requirement is to be able to predict how employees are going to behave. How many of the new entrants are going to fail training? How many (and which) employees are going to leave this year, next year and so on? How many have the capacity and the motivation to be trained or to be developed to fill posts at a higher level? (see E3). It should be clear that to be able to estimate the behaviour and capacities of personnel an assessment of their aptitudes, performance, motivation and interests is required. With estimates of the requirements for personnel and a prediction of the likely state of the work force in the future it is possible to plan and adjust the situation so that the work force meets the requirements.

✓ Manpower planning is particularly important in organizations which employ large numbers of professional and highly skilled staff. Planning is particularly critical in such organizations when the work is highly specialized and trained people outside the organization are not readily available. This is the position of many professional groups and trades in the Royal Air Force. To be operationally effective the RAF requires a number of highly trained pilots able to operate certain categories of aircraft. It takes many years for a pilot to reach operational efficiency and the effective flying life of a pilot is relatively short. The failure rate in training is also high but it can be predicted fairly accurately from information on the potential of entrants obtained in the selection situation and the relationship between such measures and performance in training from previous years.

Apart from training failures other forms of wastage must be taken into account. Estimates must be made of the number of pilots leaving at various stages of their career. This can be achieved with some degree of accuracy by the analysis of past statistics and by conducting attitude surveys of appropriate cohorts of pilots to assess whether they will stay or leave the service several years ahead. This can be done by direct questions of intention, but predictions are more accurate if attitudes to work and career, the domestic circumstances of the officer and his attitude towards alternative careers are taken into account. The use of attitude surveys in manpower planning is still in its infancy but techniques are being developed.

Planning to achieve the right number of pilots is only part of the problem. The pilots must be trained for the right aircraft and retrained or 'converted' to different aircraft from time to time during their career. The majority of senior managers and administrators in the RAF are pilots or ex-pilots, so an important aspect of career planning is to ensure that there is sufficient talent among pilot entries to the service to produce these senior officers. The careers of the senior officers also have to be planned in order that they acquire sufficient training and experience in administration and management posts to equip them for their later responsibilities.

The various aspects of the personnel system of an organization are closely interrelated. That is to say changes in one part of the system affect other posts. Changes in recruitment policy or variation in the standard of entrants has implications for training, later performance, promotability of personnel and so on. Changes in internal policy or forces external to the organization which may result in staff leaving at a faster or slower rate obviously have implications for the recruitment and training of personnel.

The rate of growth or decline in the size of an organization has a marked effect on personnel policy. Rapid expansion in a company creates opportunities for promotion and staff tend to get promoted younger. Lots of new staff have to be taken on, trained and assimilated into the company. If growth in the company ceases new positions are no longer created and as senior posts in the company are filled by relatively young men (and women) they are likely to remain in their posts for many years – thus the promotion prospects for junior staff in the company are poor. If the company starts contracting the position is made even worse. Periods of rapid growth put a strain on the personnel resources of an organization while periods of decline frustrate people who are capable of developing to more senior positions.

It is possible to analyse the age structure of personnel in large organizations and relate it to periods of growth and decline. Once an organization is seriously out of balance it may take a generation or two to correct it. Whether an organization has a predominantly young or predominantly old management is likely to have far-reaching implications for the style of the organization and its policies. For long-term survival and for effective planning a steady, slow growth in the organization is better than sudden shifts.

What is true of firms in this respect is also largely true for professions and industries. The rapid expansion of university education in the last decade has created opportunities for promotion which would not otherwise have existed. This rapid growth period has now come to an end and many academics will now retain their chairs for many years while relatively few new ones will be created.

There have been some attempts in recent years to develop mathematical models of the personnel system of organizations. The practical value of such models is that predictions can be made of the resulting effects of possible changes in the requirements of the organization due to

122

technological change or changing economic and market conditions. Most of the models to date are based upon a very simple assumption of the statistical relationships between different parts of the system. Some of the more sophisticated take into account psychological assessments of intelligence, aptitudes, performance and attitudes.

11
Future developments

Technical developments

The development of intelligence and aptitude tests has a relatively long history and there is now considerable evidence to demonstrate their value in making certain types of personnel decision. We also know the limitations of such measures. Intelligence tests are best at predicting future performance on tasks which resemble those presented in intelligence tests. That is to say, they are very useful for predicting ability at tackling problems requiring the application of inductive and deductive reasoning. Such tests are also valuable in predicting the speed of learning, particularly in academic subjects. This fact can be put to good use in selecting people for jobs involving a significant amount of training as we have seen. The accuracy with which performance in jobs can be predicted from intelligence and aptitude tests is rather lower. This is because performance in most real-life situations depends on many factors other than intelligence. Nevertheless, such tests can still be of value even if their predictability is low.

Although minor improvements may occur in the techniques of measuring of intelligence and aptitude during the next decade one cannot expect significant developments. The only important new development in cognitive testing may be in the testing of creativity. This is one area where interesting research is taking place (see A7).

The area where there is scope for making major improvements in selection is in the measurement of personality and motivation. Although it seems evident that success in many jobs is largely dependent upon drive, determination, reliability and so on, our ability to assess these characteristics is very poor (see D3). This is where the big breakthrough in selection could come. The difficulty in predicting behaviour in these respects stems largely from the fact that these characteristics, unlike intelligence, are largely situationally determined. That is to say, individuals can be highly motivated in one situation but have little motivation in another. What is thus required is to understand in some detail the needs, interests and ambitions of each individual applicant or employee to be able to predict how he will react in various situations. Judgements can then be made as to whether he will fit into the positions for which he is being considered and also to what extent the organization could respond to meeting his needs.

Psychologists have made some progress in understanding the nature of personality and motivation. Attempts to design robust measures that can be used for practical purposes for making personnel decisions have so far met with little success. The accumulating evidence of the importance of measures of introversion-extraversion and neuroticism to a variety of situations is impressive. The development of physiological and behavioural measures of these dimensions would represent a significant step forward.

The work on motivation measures by Cattell (see Chapter 3) could make an important contribution to the prediction of behaviour at work. The Motivation Analysis Test, which has been little used in this country, is only partially relevant to work behaviour but the technique could be adapted. The objective version of this test, which involves a variety of performance tests, might also be adapted for use in selection procedures.

Human resource accounting

There has been a good deal of interest during the last few years in the possibility of being able to quantify in financial terms the value to an organization of individuals with certain sets of skills. This area of interest is normally described as human resource accounting or human asset accounting. The underlying idea behind these developments is that if human assets could be quantified in this way it would be possible to plan, allocate and develop human resources in a company in a rational manner and to co-ordinate such planning with that of capital equipment. The idea is clearly attractive to senior management and accountants in particular. Even if valuing people in this way is not carried out explicitly, it must be done implicitly, determining whether it is worth employing additional staff and at what levels.

Putting a price on people's skills and calculating the return for investment in additional training and the provision of experience is proving very difficult. Individuals vary considerably in their value to the company, even when the formal qualifications may be similar. Further, it is not realistic to consider the value of an individual's skills separately from the company's capability of effectively utilizing those skills. Unlike capital equipment, companies do not own their employees and cannot retain staff against their will, nor can they sell them. The exception to this would appear to be professional footballers, who appear to be 'owned' by clubs and bought and sold. Human asset accounting to football club managers is very clearly a reality! Other organizations retain staff on contracts (e.g. the armed services, film companies in the case of film stars) and as a result may invest more money in their development than they otherwise would. The fact that employees are free to leave organizations and switch freely from one to another poses severe constraints on the nature of human asset models being developed.

The success of human resource accounting will depend on the extent to which the potential and skills of individuals can be quantified (the main theme of this book) and the extent to which these quantities can be translated into financial terms. Behavioural models of the relationships between such variables as morale and productivity must be more clearly defined (see Dermer and Siegel 1974).

Developments in human resource accounting may enable firms to better quantify the costs of high labour turnover and absenteeism, low morale and poor industrial relations. A clearer recognition of the costs of these factors may encourage more companies to consider how they organize work to involve employees and better satisfy their needs in order to reduce such costs.

The changing nature of work

The model for the selection of personnel which psychologists have developed is based upon the assumption that jobs consist of a set of clearly defined tasks. Most models of training and performance appraisal also implicitly make this assumption. With the exception of relatively unskilled jobs in factories and offices and certain manual jobs, it is seldom possible to define jobs in this way. With the advent of new forms of work organization which give employees more autonomy in how they carry out their tasks and a greater say in the way work is organized, the trend will be to less well-defined jobs even in these occupations.

The jobs of managers and professionals are defined more appropriately in terms of the objectives they should fulfil rather than the specific tasks they carry out. For example, the objective of a sales manager may be to increase sales by 10 per cent this year. He may achieve this by improving the administrative efficiency of his sales organization, by improving the morale of his sales force and motivating them to greater efforts, by improving the bonus system, by increasing the number of salesmen and so on. The skills required for each of these approaches may be different, and the cost of persons required to carry them through may differ. What then are the qualities required of the successful sales manager for this position? It would not be realistic to spell out all the sets of skills required to plan and carry out each of the approaches to the problem. What one could look for is a different level of attributes to those described earlier. For example, the sales manager would require a fairly high level of general ability and judgement to analyse the situation and select the appropriate course of action. He should also select a course of action which he can effectively carry through. This means being aware of his own skills and abilities and also being aware of his limitations. This awareness of one's own strengths and weaknesses is an important ingredient of the successful organization man. Few people have the attributes for success in a wide range of pursuits. The successful person is one who arranges situations to make the best use of those qualities he has.

It is not only people in senior positions that can shape their job to suit themselves. Most workers do this to some extent and it is entirely reasonable that they should. Effective managers are those who facilitate this process and adapt their organization to meet the needs of their staff and who develop and utilize the skills of their staff to best advantage. If a job is seen as a flexible and dynamic

128

entity it clearly has implications for the model of selection adopted.

The other reason why jobs might be perceived in this way is that technology is changing so fast that the skills required by employees are likely to change, perhaps several times, during the course of a working life. With the advent of automation certain skills become redundant while the need for new skills is often created.

If the trends described continue and all the indications suggest they will, jobs in the future will be less structured and individual employees will be required to adapt and learn new skills at various times during their working life. Selection criteria might be expected to reflect these changing requirements and concentrate less on the skills required to perform specific tasks and more on general ability, flexibility and adaptability. If employees have greater autonomy over their working situation more emphasis should also be placed in selection on initiative and the acceptance of responsibility. Training and performance appraisal should also recognize the changing nature of work and reflect these requirements.

Appendix
Statistical concepts

This appendix has been provided for readers with no knowledge of statistics. It describes the statistical concepts used in this book without going into the mathematics. A more extended coverage of statistics in psychology can be found in A8.

Normal distribution
A distribution refers to the spread of scores along a scale. A normal distribution is one in which the majority of scores cluster around the mean (average) value with a diminishing number at values either side of the mean. The normal distribution is symmetrical.

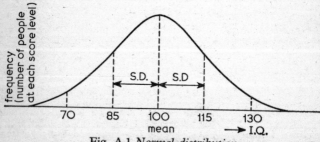

Fig. A.1 *Normal distribution*

Standard deviation (SD)

The Standard Deviation of a distribution of scores is an index of the spread of scores along the scale. In the normal distribution about one-third of the scores fall between the mean and the score at one SD from the mean. Thus two-thirds of the scorers are between the +1SD and −1SD limits. About 95 per cent of the scorers fall between the + 2SD and − 2SD limits.

Intelligence tests when tried out on a random sample of the general population (adults) are commonly converted to a normal distribution. The conversion formula is such as to produce a mean of 100 and an SD of 15. Thus two-thirds of the population falls between an IQ of 85 and 115. Ninety-five per cent fall between 70 and 130. Only $2\frac{1}{2}$ per cent score below 70 and a further $2\frac{1}{2}$ score above 130.

Correlation

The correlation between two measures is an index of the way in which they are related to each other. If the variation in one factor is directly related to the variation in a second, such as that between the length of a metal rod and its temperature, the correlation in expressed unity is ($r = +1.00$). This relationship is shown graphically in Figure A.2. A feature of this relationship is that from a knowledge

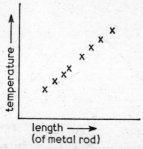

Fig. A.2 *Correlation of r = 1·0*

131

of the temperature an exact prediction of the length of the rod could be made.

If no relationship exists between two variables the correlation will be calculated as zero ($r = 0.00$). If presented graphically the points would show a random scatter (not shown).

The relationship between a good selection test and a subsequent measure of performance at work would be positive but less than perfect. Figure A.3. shows a hypothetical relationship of $r = 0.5$. Although there is a spread of scores the positive trend is evident. From a knowledge of the selection test score it is not possible to make an exact prediction of performance but an estimate can be made.

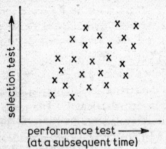

Fig. A.3 *Correlation of* $r = 0.50$

Further Reading

Anstey, Edgar (1966) *Psychological Tests.* London: Nelson.

Barrett, R. S. (1966) *Performance Rating.* Chicago, Ill.: Science Research Associates.

Blum, M. and Naylor, J. (1968) Chapters 2–6 of *Industrial Psychology.* New York: Harper International.

Cattell, R. B. (1965) *The Scientific Analysis of Personality.* Harmondsworth: Penguin.

Eysenck, H. J. (1960) *The Structure of Human Personality.* London: Routledge and Kegan Paul.

Guion, R. M. (1965) *Personnel Testing.* New York: McGraw Hill.

Hall, C. S. and Lindzey, G. (1970) *Theories of Personality.* (2nd edn) New York: Wiley.

References and Name Index

(*The numbers in italics following each reference refer to page numbers within this book.*)

Alderfer, C. P. (1969) An empirical test of a theory of human needs. *Organisational Behaviour and Human Performance* 4:142–75. *48*

Allport, G. W. and Vernon, P. E. (1970) *Study of Values* – Manual (3rd edn). New York: Houghton Mifflin. *54, 92*

Anderson, R. C. (1954) The guided interview as an evaluative instrument. *Journal of Educational Research* 48:203–9. *82, 84*

Anstey, E. (1961) *Staff Reporting and Staff Development.* London: Allen & Unwin. *74*

Applied Psychology Unit (1969) *Interests Guide* – Manual. London: University Press. *95*

Argyle, M. (1972) *The Psychology of Interpersonal Behaviour.* Harmondsworth: Penguin. *86, 87*

Armstrong, T. B. (1971) Job content and context factors related to satisfaction for different occupational levels. *Journal of Applied Psychology* 55:57–65. *49*

Atkinson, J. W. (1958) *Motives in Fantasy, Action and Society.* New York: Van Nostrand. *53, 54*

Bennett, G. K., Seashore, H. G. and Wesman, A. L. (1966) *Differential Aptitude Tests (Forms C & M) Manual.* New York: Psychological Corporation. *29, 90*

Berkshire, J. R. and Highland, R. W. (1953) Forced-choice performance rating: a methodological study. *Personnel Psychology* 6:355–78. *75*

Blewett, D. G. (1954) An experimental study of the inheritance of intelligence. *Journal of Mental Science* 100:922–33. *32*

Bogardus, E. S. (1925) Measuring social distance. *Journal of Applied Sociology* 9:229–308. *67*

Bonneau, L. R. (1957) An interview for selecting teachers. *Dis-*

sertation Abstracts 17:537–8. *84*

Burns, T. and Stalko, G. M. (1961) *The Management of Innovation*. London: Tavistock. *117*

Burt, C. (1939) The relations of educational abilities. *British Journal of Educational Psychology* 9:45–71. *23*

Campbell, D. P. (1973) The strong vocational interest blank for men. In D. G. Zytowski (ed.) *Contemporary Approaches to Interest Measurement*. Minneapolis, Minn.; University of Minnesota Press. *98*

Campbell, D. T. (1950) The indirect assessment of social attitudes. *Psychological Bulletin* 47:15–38. *67*

Cattell, R. S. (1959) *Motivation Analysis Test Manual*. Illinois: Institute for Personality and Ability Testing. *56*

Cattell, R. S. (1963) *Culture-fair Test of g* – Manual. Illinois: Institute for Personality and Ability Testing. *27*

Cattell, R. S. (1965) *The Scientific Analysis of Personality*. Harmondsworth: Penguin. *18, 35, 41*

Cattell, R. S. and Warburton, F. W. (1967) *Objective Personality and Motivation Tests*. Urbana, Ill.: Illinois Press. *43*

Chapple, E. D. (1956) *The Interaction Chronograph Manual*. Connecticut: Morton. *87*

Cowles, J. T. (1937) Food tokens as incentives for learning by chimpanzees. *Comparative Psychological Monographs* no. *14*:96. *46*

Davis, J. D. (1971) *The Interview as Arena*. Stanford, Calif.: Stanford University Press. *87*

Dermer, J. and Siegel, J. P. (1974) The role of behavioural measures in accounting for human resources. *The Accounting Review* 49:88–97. *127*

Dion, K. L., Baron, R. S. and Miller, N. (1970) Why do groups make riskier decisions than individuals? In L. Berkowitz (ed.) *Advances in Experimental Social Psychology 5*. New York: Academic Press. *80*

Doob, L. (1947) The behaviour of attitudes. *Psychological Review* 54:135–56. *58*

Ewen, R. B. (1967) Weighting components of job satisfaction. *Journal of Applied Psychology* 51:68–73. *52*

Eysenck, H. J. (1960) *The Structure of Human Personality*. London: RKP. *18, 35*

Eysenck, H. J. (1971) *Race, Intelligence and Education*. London: Temple-Smith. *31*

Eysenck, H. J. and Eysenck, S. B. G. (1964) *Manual of Eysenck Personality Inventory*. London: University Press. *42, 114*

Eysenck, H. J. and Eysenck, S. B. G. (1969) *Personality Structure and Measurement*. London: RKP. *36*

Flanagan, J. C. (1949a) Job requirements. In W. Dennis (ed.) *Current Trends in Industrial Psychology*. Pittsburgh, Pa.: University of Pittsburgh Press. *76, 105*

Flanagan, J. C. (1949b) Critical requirements: a new approach to employee evaluation. *Personnel Psychology* 2:419–25. *76, 105*

Flanagan, J. C. and Burns, R .K. (1955) The employee performance record: a new appraisal and development tool. *Harvard Business Review* 33:95–102. *76*

Galton, F. (1883) *Inquiries into Human Faculty and its Development.* London: Macmillan. *21*

General Aptitude Test Battery, B–1002, Manual (1968) Washington, D.C.: United States Department of Labor. *29–31, 90*

Georgopoulous, B. S., Mahoney, G. M. and Jones, N. W. (1957) A path-goal approach to productivity. *Journal of Applied Psychology* 41:345–53. *51*

Ghiselli, E. E. (1973) The validity of aptitude tests in personnel selection. *Personnel Psychology* 26:461–77. *40, 91*

Goldman, L. (1961) *Using Tests in Counselling.* New York: Appleton-Century-Crofts. *98*

Gorden, R. L. (1956) Dimensions of the depth interview. *American Journal of Sociology* 62:158–64. *87*

Guest, L. L. (1947) A study of interviewer competence. *International Journal of Opinion and Attitude Research* 1:17–30. *87*

Guilford, J. P. (1967) *The Nature of Human Intelligence.* New York: McGraw-Hill. *23*

Guttman, L. (1944) A basis for scaling qualitative data. *American Sociological Review* 9:139–50. *64*

Hammond, K. R. (1948) Measuring attitudes by error-choice: an indirect method. *Journal of Abnormal and Social Psychology* 43:38–48. *60*

Hardinge, N. (1974) *Civil Service Promotion Methods.* An examination of the contribution of interviews to promotion board decisions, and of the consistency of board members' judgments. *Behavioural Science Research Department Paper No. 9.* Unpublished paper by the Civil Service Department. *82*

Heim, Alice W. (1968) (1975 new edn) *AH 4–5 Group Tests of Intelligence Manuals* (rev. edn). Slough: National Foundation for Educational Research. *27*

Heller, K., Davis, J. and Myers, R. (1966) The effects of interviewer style in a standardised interview. *Journal of Consulting Psychology* 30(6):501–508. *87*

Herzberg, F. (1968) One more time – how do you motivate employees? *Harvard Business Review* 46:53–62. *48–50, 66, 92*

Holmes, J. E. (1964) The presentation of test information to college freshmen. *Journal of Counselling Psychology* 11:54–8. *98*

House, R. J. and Wigdor, L. A. (1967) Herzberg's dual-factor theory of job satisfaction and motivation: a review of the evidence and a criticism. *Personnel Psychology* 20:369–90. *48*

Hoyt, D. P. (1955) An evaluation of group and individual programs in vocational guidance. *Journal of Applied Psychology* 39:26–30. *99*

Hull, C. L. (1943) *Principles of Behaviour*. New York: Appleton-Century-Crofts. *46*

Hyman, H. H. (1944) Do they tell the truth? *Public Opinion Quarterly* 8:557–9.

James, W. (1890) *The Principles of Psychology*. New York: Holt. *46*

Jensen, A. R. (1969) Environment, heredity and intelligence. *Harvard Ed. Review Report No. 2*. *31*

Jessup, G. and Jessup, H. (1971) Validity of the Eysenck personality inventory in pilot selection. *Occupational Psychology* 45:111–23. *41, 114–5*

Jourard, S. (1971) *Self-Disclosure*. New York: Wiley. *87*

Jung, C. (1953) Quoted in Frieda Fordham, *An Introduction to Jung's Psychology*. Harmondsworth: Penguin. *35*

Kahn, R. L. and Cannell, C. F. (1957) *The Dynamics of Interviewing*. New York: Wiley *87*

Kelly, G. A. (1955) *The Psychology of Personal Constructs 1*. New York: Norton. *59*

Kelly, E. L. and Fiske, D. W. (1951) *The Prediction of Performance in Clinical Psychology* Ann Arbor, Mich.: University of Michigan Press. *83–4*

Kendon, A. (1972) Some relationships between body motion and speech: an analysis of an example. In A. Siegman and B. Pope (eds) *Studies in Dyadic Communication* Oxford: Pergamon. *87*

Krasner, L. (1958) Studies of the conditioning of verbal behaviour. *Psychological Bulletin* 55:148–70. *87*

Kretschmer, E. (1948) *Körperbau und Charackter*. Berlin: Springer. *34*

Krumboltz, J. D. and Thoresen, C. E. (1969) *Behavioural Counselling: Cases and Techniques* New York: Holt, Rinehart and Winston. *102, 103*

Kuder Vocational Preference Record Form CP. (1951) Illinois, USA: Science Research Associates. *93–4*

Lanyon (1972) In O.K. Buros, *Mental Measurements Yearbook*. *41*

La Piere, R. T. (1934) Attitudes versus actions. *Social Forum 13*: 230–7. *59*

Likert, R. (1932) A technique of the measurement of attitudes. *Archives of Psychology* 140:44–53. *64*

McClelland, D. C. (1961) *The Achieving Society*. New York: Van Nostrand. *48*

McDougall, W. (1923) *Outline of Psychology*. New York: Scribner. *46*

Maslow, A. (1970) *Motivation and Personality* (2nd edn). New York: Harper & Row. *47–8*

Mayfield, E. C. (1964) The selection interview – A re-evaluation of published research. *Personnel Psychology* 17:239–60. *82–3, 88*

Mehrabian, A. and Diamond, S. (1971) Seating arrangement and conversation. *Sociometry 34*:281–9. *86*

Murray, H. A. (1943) (1971) *Thematic Apperception Test Manual.* Cambridge, Mass.: Harvard University Press. *38, 53, 92*

Nelson, D. M. (1968) The predictive value of the Rothwell–Miller interest blank. *Occupational Psychology 42*:123–31. *95*

Osgood, C. E., Suci, G. J. and Tannenbaum, P. H. (1957) *The Measurement of Meaning.* Chicago, Ill.: University of Illinois Press. *60*

Otis, J. L., Campbell, J. H. and Prien, E. D. (1962) Assessment of higher-level personnel VII: the nature of assessment. *Personnel Psychology 15*:441–6. *84–5*

Patterson, C. H. (1969) What is counselling psychology? *Journal of Counselling Psychology 16*:23–9. *101*

Pilato, G. T. (1968) The effects of three vocational guidance treatments on some aspects of vocational preference and self knowledge. Unpublished doctoral dissertation. Columbia University. Quoted by Myers, R. A. in *Handbook of Psychotherapy and Behaviour Change.* Allen E. Bergin and Sol. L. Garfield (eds) New York: Wiley, 1971. *99*

Poppleton, P. K. and Pilkington, G. W. (1964) A comparison of four methods of scoring an attitude scale in relation to its reliability and validity. *British Journal of Social and Clinical Psychology 3*:36–9. *64*

Porter, L. W. (1962) Job attitudes in management I: perceived deficiencies in need fulfilment as a function of job level. *Journal of Applied Psychology 46*:375–84. *48*

Porter, L. W. (1963) Job attitudes in management II: perceived importance of needs as a function of job level. *Journal of Applied Psychology 47*:141–8. *48*

Porter, L. W. and Lawler, E. E. (1968) *Managerial Attitudes and Performance.* Homewood, Illinois: Irwin-Dorsey. *51*

Rambo, W. W. (1959) The effects of partial pairing on scale values derived from the method of paired comparisons. *Journal of Applied Psychology 43*:379–81. *71*

Raven, J. C. (1958) *Raven's Standard Matrices.* London: H. K. Lewis. *26, 56*

Richardson, S., Dohrenwend, B. and Klein, D. (1965) *Interviewing, its Forms and Functions.* New York: Basic Books. *87*

Rimland, B. (1960) Quoted in Ulrich, L. and Trumbo, D., The selection interview since 1949. *Psychological Bulletin 1965 63*: 100–16. *84*

Rodger, A. and Cavanagh, P. (1962) *Personnel Selection and Vocational Guidance in Society. Problem and Methods of Study.* A. T. Welford (ed) London: Routledge and Kegan Paul. *89, 102*

Rogers, C. R. (1952) Client-centred psychotherapy. *Scientific/*

American Reprints November 1952. Reading: W. H. Freeman & Co. *102*

Rorschach Technique Introductory Manual (1962) B. Klopfer and H. Davidson (eds) New York: Harcourt-Brace. *37*

Rothwell–Miller Interest Blank (1968) NFER Publishing Company Limited. *93*

Rowe, Kay H. (1964) An appraisal of appraisals. *Journal of Management Studies 1*:1–25. *75*

Salzinger, K. and Pisoni, S. (1960) Reinforcement of verbal affect responses of normal subjects during an interview. *Journal of Abnormal and Social Psychology 60*:127–30. *87*

Schachter, S. (1959) *The Psychology of Affiliation.* Stanford, Calif.: Stanford University Press. *47*

Scott, W. D. (1915) Quoted in E. C. Mayfield (1964). *82*

Shaw, J. (1952) The function of the interview in determining fitness for teacher training. *Journal of Educational Research 45*:667–81. *82*

Sheldon, W. H. (1940) *The Varieties of Human Physique.* New York: Harper. *34*

Sisson, E. D. (1948) Forced-choice: the new army rating. *Personnel Psychology* Vol. 1. 365–81 *75*

Skeels, H. M. and Dye, H. B. (1939), A study of the effects of differential stimulation. *Proceedings of the American Association for Mental Deficiency 44*:114–36. *32*

Smith, P. C., Kendall, L. M. and Hulin, C. L. (1969) *The Measurement of Satisfaction in Work and Retirement.* Skokie, Ill.: Rand McNally. *65*

Spearman, C. (1927) *Abilities of Man.* New York: Macmillan. *22*

Stefflre, B. (1965) Function and present status of counselling theory. In B. Stefflre (ed.) *Theories of Counselling.* New York: McGraw-Hill. *103*

Stern (1938). Quoted in B. Dohrenwend, S. Richardson and D. Klein *Interviewing: Its Forms and Functions.* New York: Basic Books, 1965. *87*

Strong Vocational Interests Blank (1969) Supplement to the Manual. Stanford, Calif.: Stanford University Press. *96–7*

Super, D. E. (1973) The work values inventory. In D. G. Zytowski (1973). *92*

Super, D. E. and Crites, J. O. (1962) *Appraising Vocational Fitness* (revised edn) New York: Harper & Row. *89, 92*

Taylor, H. C. and Russell, J. T. (1939) The relationship of validity co-efficients to the practical effectiveness of tests in selection: Discussion and tables. *Journal of Applied Psychology 23*:565–78. *110*

Thomson, G. H. (1951) *The Factorial Analysis of Human Ability* (5th edn) Boston, Mass.: Houghton Mifflin. *109*

Thurstone, L. L. (1928) Attitudes can be measured. *American*

Journal of Sociology 33:529–54. *63*

Thurstone, L. L. (1938) Primary mental abilities. *Psychometric Monographs 1*. *23*

Thurstone, T. G., Thurstone, L. L. and Strandskov, H. H. (1953) A psychological study of twins. *Psychometric Laboratory Report no 4*. Chapel Hill: University of California. *32*

Tipton, R. M. (1969) Relative effectiveness of two methods of interpreting ability test scores. *Journal of Counselling Psychology 16*:75–80. *99*

Tittle, C. R. and Hill, R. J. (1967) Attitude measurement and prediction of behaviour: an evaluation of conditions and measurement techniques. *Sociometry 30*:199–213. *64*

Triandis, H. C. (1959) Categories of thought of managers, clerks and workers about jobs and people in industry. *Journal of Applied Psychology 43*:338–44. *60*

Triandis, H. C. (1971) *Attitudes and Attitude Change*. New York: Wiley. *61*

Uhrbrock, R. S. (1961) 2,000 scaled items. *Personnel Psychology 14*:375–420. *63*

Ulrich, L. and Trumbo, D. (1965) The selection interview since 1949. *Psychological Bulletin 63*:100–16. *81, 82*

Vernon, P. E. (1961) *The Structure of Human Abilities*. London: Methuen. *23, 24*

Vernon, P. E. (1969) *Intelligence and Cultural Environment*. London: Methuen. *31*

Veroff, J., Atkinson, J. W., Feld, S. C. and Gurin, G. (1960) The use of thematic apperception to assess motivation in a nation-wide interview study. *Psychological Monographs 74*:No. 12. *48*

Vroom, V. (1964) *Work and Motivation*. New York: Wiley. *50*

Webb, E. J., Campbell, D. T., Schwartz, R. D and Sechrest, L. (1966) *Unobtrusive Measures*. Skokie, Ill.: Rand McNally. *67*

Weber, M. (1947) *The Theory of Social and Economic Organization*. N.Y.: Free Press. *117*

Whyte, W. H. (1963) *The Organization Man*. New York: Simon & Schuster, 1956. Pelican, 1963. *39, 54*

Williams, J. E. and Hills, D. A. (1962) More on brief educational vocational counselling. *Journal of Counselling Psychology 9*:366–8. *99*

Winterbottom, M. R. (1958) The relation of need for achievement to learning experiences in independence and mastery. In J. W. Atkinson (1958). *47*

Zaccaria, M. A. *et al.* (1956) Quoted in L. Ulrich and D. Trumbo (1965). *82*

Zytowski, D. G. (1973) The Kuder Occupational Interest Survey. In D. G. Zytowski (ed.) *Contemporary Approaches to Interest Measurement*. Minneapolis, Minn.: University of Minnesota Press. *101*

Subject Index